RIDE OF A LIFETIME

RIDE OF A
LIFETIME

THE
SANDY HAWLEY
STORY

Sandy Hawley and Perry Lefko

Fenn Publishing Company Ltd.
Bolton, Canada

RIDE OF A LIFETIME
A Fenn Publishing Book / First Published in 2005

Fenn Publishing Company Ltd.
Bolton, Ontario, Canada

Distributed in Canada by H. B. Fenn and Company Ltd.
Bolton, Ontario, Canada, L7E 1W2
www.hbfenn.com

Library and Archives Canada Cataloguing in Publication

Hawley, Sandy, 1949-
    Ride of a lifetime : the Sandy Hawley story / Sandy Hawley
and Perry Lefko.

Includes index.
ISBN 1-55168-271-0

1. Hawley, Sandy, 1949- 2. Jockeys--Canada--Biography.
I. Lefko, Perry II. Title.

SF336.H39A3 2005   798.4'0092   C2005-903025-9

Printed and bound in Canada

DEDICATION

To the memories of my mentor, Duke Campbell; my mother, Gloria Hawley; and my father-in-law, Isaac John. And to my wife, Lisa; my two sons, Bradley and Russell; my father, Des; my mother-in-law, Monica; and jockey agent Colin Wick. Each of you has a special place in my heart.

Sandy Hawley

To Jerry Gladman, one of the most influential people in my career as a journalist and author. He was not only a good writer, but a real *mensch*.

Perry Lefko

ACKNOWLEDGEMENTS

Thanks to Jordan Fenn of Fenn Publishing for accepting the idea for this book and to Woodbine Entertainment Group (formerly the Ontario Jockey Club) for its support. Thanks also to literary agent Arnold Gosewich, who worked tirelessly to put both parties together while also working with the authors, and to Glenn Crouter, the extraordinary director of media communications for the Woodbine Entertainment Group, for facilitating the project. The authors are grateful to Lloyd Davis of Lloyd Davis Communications and Jim Bannon of Woodbine Entertainment Group for their work in editing the manuscript. Thanks to Jim Jennings and Julie Kirsh of the *Toronto Sun* for guidance and support.

There are many people who offered their time for interviews, while others provided data, newspaper clippings or phone numbers. Thanks to Colin Wick, Des Hawley, Lisa Hawley, Sherrie Hawley, John Tyre, Jack Wood, Ronnie Robinson, Bob Benoit, Marje Everett, Dr. Malcolm Mitchell, Gordon Jones, David Willmot, Bobby Frankel, Gary Jones, Lou Cavalaris, Jim Bannon, Nat Wess, Larry Bortstein, John Siscos, Lou Cauz, John DeSantis, Chick McLellan, Scotty McLellan, Laffit Pincay, Chris McCarron, Joe Hawk, Tony Pinessa, Richard Eng, Steve and Jennifer Lym, Peter Walder, George and Nina Williams, Richard Depass, *The California Thoroughbred*, the *Daily Racing Form*'s Bill Tallon and Karen Shaw, Keeneland Racetrack and the *Toronto Sun*.

Special thanks to Kimberly Kasper of Interactive Offices Worldwide and Vanessa Milne of the *Toronto Sun* for their transcribing help.

Co-author Perry Lefko would like to especially thank his wife, Jane, and two children, Ben and Shayna, for their patience

CONTENTS

PREFACE

Unquestionably the outstanding individual athlete in Canada today is a 27-year-old, 110-pound jockey who, out at the Woodbine racetrack, is adding a brilliant new chapter to our country's sporting history. Some years ago, Bruce Hutchison wrote a biography entitled *The Incredible Canadian*. The subject of Mr. Hutchison's biography was the Right Honourable W.L. Mackenzie King, who established an all-time endurance record as prime minister of our benighted land. With all due deference to Mr. Hutchison and the ghost of Mackenzie King, it's high time that some budding sports historian stole that same title, *The Incredible Canadian*, for a biography of jockey Sandford Hawley.

Journalist *Jim Coleman*, October 1976

FOREWORD

The thing that comes to mind most when I think about Sandy Hawley is his love of life. He really knows how to have a good time.

Sandy is extremely competitive — not just on the track, but also on the golf course or playing Ping Pong or a game of cards. We used to have Ping Pong tournaments all the time in the jocks' room and he was always one of the organizers. He had to win at everything, and he usually did. I think that's one of his endearing and admirable qualities, aside from the fact he's also got an awesome sense of humour.

In 1973, when he broke Bill Shoemaker's world record of 485 wins in a season on Charlie Jr. at Laurel Race Course, I was at the races that day, standing in the crowd behind the winner's circle. (I was an exercise rider at the time.) I kept leaping up in the air, trying to hold on to a big guy's shoulder, hoping that when Sandy crossed the finish line and the photographer snapped the picture, I'd be part of the historic photo. Unfortunately, that didn't work out for me, but a year later I *was* in the picture — my own picture, when I broke Sandy's record of 515 winners.

I rode in my first race on January 24, 1974, and won for the first time on February 9. By the end of March I had somewhere between 20 and 30 winners. Then we moved over to Pimlico and I broke the record with 113 winners in 60 days; my agent mentioned that if we continued at that pace, we would have a shot at Sandy's record. I looked at him as if he'd been drinking his bathwater. I rode seven cards a week from May until September, when I added a card by riding at Penn National, two hours away, after riding at Laurel on Saturdays. So, from the end of September until the end of the year, I was riding eight cards a week.

Years later, Sandy and I talked about my breaking his record. I remember thanking him for moving to California in 1975 because that — along with Vincent Bracciale leaving Maryland for New York and Darrel McHargue going to California — opened a lot of doors for me in '74.

In 1978 I moved to California to ride full time, and it was around 1979 or '80 that I developed a friendship with Sandy. He invited me to start playing golf with him and his buddies — Dean Scarborough, Jack Wood and John Tyre — who got together every Monday or Tuesday. I'd never been much into golf as a kid, but my dad was, and my eldest brother, Joe, was a teaching pro for a while.

I just naturally had the desire and interest to take it up. I think it was the fun we had on the golf course that caused Sandy and me to become fast friends.

Sandy also helped me become a better rider, simply by competing against me on a daily basis. He could do some magical things on a horse, and all one had to do was watch and learn. Moreover, if you were not sure about something, you only had to ask him; he was always willing to share his philosophies and ideas on how to get the best out of horses. He made everyone around him a better rider.

I was honoured when Sandy chose me to be his best man at his wedding in 1983. It was a lovely event, that's for sure. It was beautiful and everybody had a wonderful time.

It was a very sad day when Sandy was diagnosed with cancer in 1986. I offered him moral support, encouragement and lots of prayers. I say a prayer every day, and I include those friends and loved ones who need the extra spiritual help. Sandy is always on my mind as far as that goes. I think the way he has been able to fight it off has been unbelievable. I would expect nothing less from a competitor such as Sandy.

I wasn't surprised when he decided to return to Canada to ride full time in 1988. He'd mentioned to me several times that, when he retired from riding, he'd like to return. Sandy is well respected everywhere he rode, but he's a hero up in Toronto. He's an icon. It was a given that he'd be able to get back up there and get his business going again.

A couple of weeks before Sandy rode his final race, in 1998, he was invited to compete with eleven other riders, including myself, in the National Thoroughbred Racing Association All-Star Jockey Challenge at Lone Star Park in Texas. I just thought it was a great way for him to go out. It would have been a travesty for such a race to take place on the North American continent without Sandy Hawley taking part. It would have been awesome for him to win the thing — that would have been the *pièce de résistance* — but to have him invited and participate was a very, very good way for him to wrap up his career.

Needless to say, Sandy Hawley has much to be proud of.

Chris McCarron,
Hall of Fame jockey,
two-time Kentucky Derby winner

INTRODUCTION

The late Jim Coleman, one of the deans of Canadian sports journalism and the author of the classic horse racing book *Hoofprints On My Heart*, would be proud. Finally, there is a book about the life and times of Sandy Hawley. It just took a little time.

I approached Sandy about doing a book during my 10-year stint covering thoroughbred races in Toronto, which began in 1987, and continued to do so after I'd moved on to other assignments. To put it mildly, he showed lukewarm interest. The fact that I hadn't exactly endeared myself to him with some of my reporting probably didn't help him warm to the idea. But independent of that, he had no desire to do a book until after his career had ended.

After his retirement in 1998 — and the prodding of many racing fans — Sandy finally became interested in the idea. I'm glad he decided to do it. As I discovered in working with him on this project, he's had a fascinating career and a remarkable life; the two have been intertwined in a series of highs and lows, both on and away from the racetrack. He has accomplished many things, yet also suffered many hardships. Ultimately, he came out on top, overcoming a battle with skin cancer and finally finding happiness as a husband in his third marriage and, subsequently, fatherhood.

In the end, this is the story of an icon who contributed greatly to the culture of Canadian sports, but who views himself as just an ordinary human being.

This is his journey, his life — the ride of a lifetime.

Perry Lefko, 2005

CHAPTER ONE

Growing Up

The journey to where I am today has truly been the ride of a lifetime, and when I reflect on it, one feeling recurs again and again. I feel very fortunate — first and foremost, to have had the career and the life that I've had. When I think about the fact I was diagnosed at one point with cancer and thought I might only have a couple of months to live, I feel very lucky to be alive and well and married with a healthy, happy family. I've enjoyed everything that's happened in my life. Sure, there have been some ups and downs, but that's part of it. There are things that you wish you could have done in your career, but I'm grateful for what has happened. It's not only about my three decades of riding, but everything that came before and after.

I was born on April 16, 1949, and named Desmond after my father, Des, but he and my mother, Gloria, started calling me Sandy, a short form of my middle name, Sandford. During my horse-racing career, I was also known as San Man. Some people even named horses after me, including one, Brilliant Sandy, that did decently and that I rode a few times.

I was born in Oshawa, Ontario, about an hour's drive east of Woodbine Racetrack, where my racing career would begin in 1968 and end thirty years later. Oshawa is where both my parents were born, and, as it turned out, the place where my soul mate, Lisa, moved to from Trinidad at the age of seven. We didn't really know one another growing up, but our paths did cross briefly in 1978. It's funny how things turn out…but more about that later.

Oshawa was home to about 45,000 people in those days — and approximately 146,000 today. Its roots date back to the early eighteenth century — the French established a trading post near the mouth of Oshawa Creek about 1750 and traded furs with the natives of the Mississauga nation. Roughly 150 years later, the town became prominent in the automotive industry when Colonel Robert Samuel McLaughlin, who had operated a local carriage works since the 1870s, began building automobiles powered by Buick engines. In 1915, he acquired the rights to build Chevrolets, and three years later the McLaughlin Motor Car Company and the Chevrolet Motor Car Company merged to form General Motors of Canada.

Famous for motorized transport, Oshawa has also played a prominent role in the history of horse racing. Colonel McLaughlin bred and raced horses there, including Horometer, who ranks as one of the greatest thoroughbreds in Canadian history. Horometer won eight of nine career races, notably the 1934 King's Plate (as the Queen's Plate is known when the reigning monarch is male). His post-time odds of 1–20 remain the lowest in the more than 140 years that the race has been run. McLaughlin won the Plate twice more, and later had a race named after him. In 1950, he sold his property, which he had named Parkwood Stable, to Edward Plunkett (E.P.) Taylor, who subsequently renamed it the National Stud Farm — and later, Windfields Farm. Taylor built it into the premier commercial breeding operation in North America, largely on the strength of the legendary Northern Dancer, who sired some of the greatest horses in the world, some of whom I had the good fortune of riding. At about the same time that Mr. Taylor moved Northern Dancer to the United States to maximize his marketability, I was in the first full year of my career.

Oshawa was a wonderful place to grow up. I don't ever recall any incidents of violence or safety or security issues back then. I was an only child — as a baby I had colic, and my mother said she was afraid to have another baby because it might be as colicky as I had been. We lived across from my cousin, Tim Keetch; he was a couple of years younger than me, but we were extremely close. In fact, he was my best friend. In the summers, beginning at the age of five or six, I'd go to his parents' cottage in Huntsville, about a two-hour drive north of Toronto.

My dad worked as a machinist in the research lab at Duplate, a company that manufactured glass. I remember the excitement of accompanying my mother in our car to pick him up. My dad missed his calling a few times in life; he should have been either a carpenter or a handyman with his own shop. He was a tremendous craftsman and builder, and he could fix his own car if it broke down. He once made a skate sharpener out of an old washing-machine motor. I still have a chess set he made me.

My mother stayed at home and did a wonderful job of raising me. She was a fantastic cook and baker, and she always kept our house so neat and clean. When I first started going to school, my mother would accompany me, but I never wanted to stay. My mother would recall that she'd arrive back home and go in through the front door just I was coming in through the back door, and she'd have to turn around and take me back. I really didn't enjoy being at school.

I was a little bit shy, probably because I was an only child. My dad was, too, but my mother was one of thirteen children. As a result, any time I rode and was assigned post position number 13, or had anything to do with the number, I always considered it lucky. But being an only child didn't mean I led a solitary life: I always had friends in the neighbourhood, and they were always over at my house — we'd go in one door and out the other. I also had tons of cousins and aunts and uncles. Our place seemed to be the focal point for Christmases and parties and get-togethers.

I have an early, very clear recollection of riding the mechanical horse outside the local Woolworths. Anytime I went past that horse, my mother would indulge me. If she had a dime or a nickel or whatever it took to operate the horse, she'd put it in the slot. But even if she didn't have any change, she'd let me sit on it while she went about her shopping. I'd just sit on the thing, pretend I was riding it and pat it on the neck as though it was a real horse. I really enjoyed those days. I felt very comfortable sitting on the horse, and the more I was on it the more comfortable I felt. It was even better when Mom put a coin in the slot; then I'd feel like I was actually riding.

I have a pretty good scar over my right eye from an accident in my youth. There was this wheelbarrow on display in front of a hardware store; it was filled with grain. My cousin, Lornie Campbell, and I were having fun on a tricycle — he was riding it and I was on the back, with one foot on board and the other kind of pushing it along. I guess my foot must have hit the wheel, because I lost my balance and fell off. One of the handles of the wheelbarrow cut my eye wide open. I ran all the way home. My parents were afraid that I might lose the eye. They took me to the hospital and the surgeon who examined me had his doubts, too. Fortunately, the damage wasn't that severe. Still, I had to wear a patch for about two weeks, and I remember being upset about it because my aunt had planned to give about four or five of us money to go to the movies, and now I couldn't go!

My best friend around that time — and I still keep in touch with him — was Fred Ruck. We used to go to the movies a lot on the weekends because we were living downtown and there weren't a lot of parks. If we wanted to play baseball or something, we'd have to go to a parking lot and hit the ball around. That sticks in my mind very clearly.

My parents had been renting the basement of a house near the main intersection in Oshawa. Then, when I was six, we moved to a new residential neighbourhood about three miles away, in Whitby. It was so new that there was nothing there, just a gravel road. Ours was only the sixth house built in the whole area, and it was surrounded by farmers' fields. The builder had dug the basement and constructed the framework, leaving it to my maternal grandfather, who was a masonry tradesman, and my father to finish the interior. While they completed the house, we lived at my aunt and uncle's place for a couple of months. Across the road there was a huge farm owned by a family named Boyd, who had cattle and workhorses, and according to my dad, I'd get up on them the odd time. I don't really recall doing it — I was more into playing hockey and softball — but I do remember watching the replays of the horse races on a TV station from Hamilton. Sometimes they'd also interview the jockeys. I'd actually be excited to come home from school to watch the show. But at this point I wasn't even thinking about becoming a jockey.

Every Friday night a bunch of us would go skating at the Whitby Arena — my dad would drive us there. He was the coach of our softball team, the Thickson Road BP's, which was sponsored by the corner gas station. I played first base, and one day during warmups one of my teammates threw a ball to me. Because of my size, it went over my head and, unfortunately, it hit my Aunt Billy, who was sitting in the stands. She wasn't looking and it hit her right in the eye. She had to be taken home by my mother, who took a steak out of the freezer and put it on the injured eye — they used to do that back then, to reduce the swelling. Aunt Billy ended up with a pretty good bruise. I felt terribly about it, but I had to stay there and finish playing the game. I think my dad ended up eating the steak for dinner the next day.

All of my mother's siblings lived in Oshawa or Whitby while I was growing up, although some of them moved to the west coast in later years. Everyone was pretty well within driving distance, and it always seemed that when there was going to be a party, it was at our house. I loved that, and to this day my wife, Lisa, and I host a New Year's Eve party at our house just about every year and have all the relatives over. We've kind of taken over from where my parents left off, and our kids love that, too. They love company, they love having relatives over. It almost reminds me of my own childhood.

My first real experiences riding horses came in the summers in Huntsville, at my aunt and uncle's cottage. I guess I was about eight or nine, and my father and uncle would take my cousin Tim and me riding. We still have home movies — now on video — of it. On one occasion, my horse was falling behind the pack and I was kicking him in the ribs trying to get him going — I didn't know too much about riding at that time. The lead rider came back and whacked my horse in the butt with his reins, and my horse just took off, flying past everyone else. Now, I couldn't get him to stop! I remember being scared, but you know what? It didn't stop me from riding. I kind of just put it behind me, and couldn't wait for the next time.

I was always the smallest in my class, but it never stopped me from playing sports. I guess I wasn't all that aware of my size: people really didn't make fun of it, so I never gave it a second thought. My Uncle Ed was a home-movie buff, and later, watching those films, I couldn't believe how much smaller I really was than everybody else. In baseball, I played first base and — just like the time my Aunt Billy was hit in the eye — the ball would sail over my head. Like any kid who grew up in Canada, I wanted to play in the National Hockey League when I grew up. Oshawa had a Major Junior A team, the Generals, who produced many NHLers, most notably the great Bobby Orr, whom I got to know really well in later years. But I knew that becoming a hockey player wasn't going to happen for me, mainly because of my size. Everyone else kept growing and I didn't. I played goal in hockey, and I was down below the crossbar.

Fred Ruck, Dieter Kerner, Johnny Greaves and I were like the four amigos. We were nearly inseparable. We used to play baseball and hockey together. We'd play softball and split up, two on two. One guy would be the pitcher and the other would be the fielder. We'd pair off for hockey, too, whether it was ball hockey or on the frozen pond at the end of the street.

It was just a fantastic childhood growing up on Thickson Road, which was like living in the country back then. Moving from the middle of Oshawa was a great decision on my parents' part. I could go out and do these things because there were fields all over the place. We used to even play home-run derby in my backyard with a bunch of the other kids. I remember when one time we were arguing who was going to be on whose team, and my dad came out and grabbed me by the back of the neck and lifted me off the ground and carried me into the house. I guess he couldn't take all the kids screaming in the backyard any longer. "The baseball game is over," he announced. We broke a lot of the windows in the house playing ball. Guys would swing and the fielder wouldn't catch it and it would sail through a ground-floor window. My dad was endlessly fixing broken windows.

I also loved playing lacrosse, and I'd bounce an India-rubber ball against the wall for hours on end. My grandfather would throw the ball to me and I'd catch it in my net and throw it back. I could catch and throw well enough, and eventually I wanted to play on a team. I played in one game and just kept getting knocked down and pushed around. I was just too small, so my dad said I couldn't play on a lacrosse team. It was very disappointing, but when I look back I wonder what ever possessed me to try it in the first place. The kids were easily twice my size!

Every winter, my dad would build a rink in our backyard. The first year, I was wearing bob skates with double blades. My dad would play hockey with me, and I wanted to play goal, so he bought me pads and put me in net. He would take shots on me, never raising the puck — though one time he did a little flip so I could catch it in my glove, and it hit me in the head. I went down and he carried me into the house, where my mom freaked out because I had a little bump on my head.

The rink my dad built wasn't really that big — it was more or less a place for me to learn how to skate and play around — but there used to be a pond down the road in a field that froze every year. When I got a little bit older, I played with the guys in the neighbourhood. We used to play almost every night — when it was dark you could still see well enough to play hockey. The "boards" consisted simply of the snow, which we'd pack up on either side. One day, I was trying to dig the puck out of one of these snow piles, and my stick caught me right in the kidney. I remember lying on the ice, doing snow angels, for quite a while.

I am a huge hockey fan. I guess that comes from my dad, who loved the Toronto Maple Leafs. I became a Leafs fan, too. I remember loving everything about hockey — playing it, watching on television, and collecting hockey cards and the little coins that used to come in boxes of Jell-O powder.

Tommy Parker was the real athlete in our public school. I was a bit envious of him because he had the size, the build and the skill. I thought he was so cool. He ended up playing junior hockey, but he never made it to the NHL. There was another kid, Billy Macdonald, who lived on the street behind me and was just a little bit bigger. We both started at Anderson High School at the same time and were good friends. He went out for the senior football team — there wasn't a junior team — and I decided I wanted to try out for the team, too. I hadn't given much thought to what position I might play — I was really fast and, given my overall athleticism, I might be able to cut it as a receiver. All I knew was that I wanted to make the team. I'd have played anywhere they wanted me to.

Billy made the team — barely. Meanwhile, I went out for two practices, after which the coach came to me and said, "I'm sorry. If we had a junior team, you'd make it, but we only have a senior team." Billy ended up riding the bench a lot, but at least he made the team. Even if I'd been a bench warmer, just knowing I'd made the team would have been satisfying enough. Now that I look back, I can see the coach's point. I couldn't have been a defender because I was too short. I couldn't really be a receiver because I'm too short. I couldn't be a running back because I wasn't big enough. I certainly couldn't play on the line! I was disappointed, but I later understood that the coach was looking out for me — he didn't want me to get hurt. As it is, I didn't play any sports at all that year. We didn't have a softball team, and I *knew* I couldn't play basketball.

In Grade 10, my buddy Fred Ruck suggested that I try out for the wrestling team. I thought it was a great idea; they had a 98-pound weight class, so I ended up wrestling in that class, although I only weighed about 94 pounds. I finished second that year in the all-Ontarios, and the guy who beat me had been wrestling for three years.

That same year, during the two-week spring vacation, the school advised my parents that it would be a good idea if I tried working at a job placement. I put my name in at a couple of grocery stores to stock shelves and that sort of thing and applied for a job at Sklar's, a furniture manufacturer that had a factory outlet near us. Sklar's allowed me to work for a week. My uncle, Web Bride, God rest his soul, went to the racetrack about once a month — sometimes every two weeks — and thought I had the right size to be a jockey. He suggested that I put my name in at the racetrack, and he called the National Stud Farm in Oshawa and asked to speak with E.P. Taylor — he must not have realized the Mr. Taylor had a busy schedule with his various businesses and might not even be there. My uncle didn't get through to Taylor, but he was told there was a trainer who boarded horses on the property in addition to those he stabled at the racetrack. We could meet with him if we wanted to arrange a visit, he was told. The trainer was Donald Hargrave (Duke) Campbell, and he would become the greatest influence on my horse-racing career.

The next day, my uncle and I met Mr. Campbell, who had grown up in Alberta and was then a veteran of more than thirty years in the business. After meeting me, he said, "Let me see your hands." He also looked down at my feet. He noticed I had small hands and small feet and remarked, "If you want to come back, we'll see what we can do. If you want to go to the racetrack for a week, that's fine. You can come out with me."

I was sixteen, and my parents were skeptical about my going to Woodbine Racetrack at that age, but once they met Duke Campbell, who was a real gentleman, they agreed to let me try it.

Des Hawley:
We said that if he progressed quite well at the track he could probably stay out there and make a career out of it. He had liked riding, and sort of liked horses in general. It just took off from there.

My time around racetracks had begun. For the next week, Mr. Campbell picked me up every morning on his way from the National Stud Farm to Woodbine. When I first went to the track, I knew one end of the horse from the other, but that's about it. "You're not going to groom horses right away," Duke told me. "I'm going to have you hot walk horses, but mainly you'll just go around the barn, and if somebody needs something done you can help them out." He wanted me to learn a few of the odd jobs first.

One of the stablehands said to me, "I want you to fill a hay net." I had no idea what a hay net was. It's a net made out of rope that you stuff with hay. It's attached to the stall door so when the horse is standing up he can nibble at it. The stablehand actually had to show me — that's how green I was. But I quickly learned what a hay net was and how to fill it.

Duke Campbell started me off brushing and taking care of the stable pony, Henry. I'll never forget his name. He was big and wide. While Duke had the pony out with the horses for their morning training session, he had me clean out Henry's stall and bed it down. "First," he said, "I want you to put some fresh straw in, and then I want you to put in some fresh hay." I remember cleaning out the whole stall, then spreading the fresh straw all around. One of the other grooms came around and said, "Why did you spread the hay all over the place? You're not supposed to do that."

"Mr. Campbell told me to bed it down with hay and straw," I said.

The stablehand went in and took all the hay off the top and corrected my mistake by piling it in the corner. This way, the horse knows where his food is; if you spread the hay all over the place it gets mixed in with the straw. What can I say? I didn't know any better.

I was a little bit intimidated at first around the horses, but I can't remember a time when I really got afraid of them as I walked them. Sometimes they'd jump around and you'd have to be careful, but I felt pretty comfortable around horses right off the bat.

It fascinated me to watch the grooms get the horses ready for the afternoon races, as they brushed the horses and made them look beautiful. Meanwhile, my job was to get Henry the stable pony nice and clean, because he'd be stained all over from lying down in the stall. He needed to be spick and span because he accompanied all of Duke Campbell's horses onto the track. It's different these days: most tracks have horses available to pony the racehorses onto the track, to help settle them down. That reminds me of a funny story that will illustrate just how green I was.

We were shipping to Greenwood, the racetrack that used to be in Toronto's east end, and a stablehand told me Henry was going to go with the horses to run in a race, and that I was to accompany him while the grooms went with the racehorses. Here's this big, huge, wide pony that probably wouldn't even fit in a starting gate, yet when I was told he was going to race I believed it! There I was, getting him nice and clean and brushed up, and I took him into the trailer with the horses who were going to race. It wasn't until the last minute that the stablehand told me Henry wasn't going to run — he was just going to pony the horses. The joke was on me.

Duke would have an exercise boy ride the pony, and the job of saddling the racehorse came with it. When I finally learned how to ride, I had to pony the horses in the afternoon. I still had this duty, even after I started racing: I'd ride in the afternoon, and if we had another horse racing later in the card and I wasn't on it, I'd have to run back to the barn and get Henry ready to pony another horse. I was probably the only jockey doing that, but for other novice riders it was a form of punishment for erring in a race. In fact, it doesn't happen very often these days — if at all, and certainly not at the major racetracks.

My parents instilled in me the importance of respecting elders, so when I addressed anyone older than me I'd call them Mr. or Mrs. or Miss. It earned me the nickname "The Gentleman Jockey." Even today, when I see the former trainer Lou Cavalaris, I call him Mr. Cavalaris. Or if I see the trainers Jerry Meyer or John Calhoun, I call them Mr. Meyer or Mr. Calhoun. A number of these individuals have told me just to call them by their first name, but it's a hard habit to overcome. It goes both ways. People will call me Mr. Hawley, and I'll tell them there's no need — just call me Sandy. Then, the next time they see me, it's "Hi, Mr. Hawley."

After my week at the racetrack, I knew I would much rather work outdoors with horses than work in a factory. When I went back to school I told all my friends, "Next year I'm going to Woodbine and I'm going to try to become a jockey." It's funny when I think about that now.

When I went back that summer, Duke Campbell had me grooming five horses. It was tough. I'd have to clean five stalls, get the horses ready. He just threw me right in there, which forced me to learn a lot right off the bat. I didn't even know how to put a saddle on a horse. It would be a little frustrating sometimes for the exercise riders, who'd be expecting the saddle to be on the horse and ready to go. But I'd often have to ask the exercise boy for help putting the saddle on. I also learned how to muck out stalls. And this was probably the easy part, but I also had to learn to work with the horses' legs, rubbing on the liniment and then putting on bandages. It was great experience, great exposure, to be around the horses and working with them.

Duke was a big, strong man who always wore a cowboy hat. To me, he was almost like John Wayne. He was very tough, too: I remember that, anytime someone around the barn would start acting up, all Duke had to do was roar at him and everybody would back down. He used to sit in the tack room and tell us stories about his days on the west coast, before he came to Ontario. He'd talk about the various jobs he'd worked at, such as being a butcher, a cattleman, a barber and even a champion boxer in Winnipeg. He used to walk around the shedrow, and every once in a while he'd reach down with his elbows and hitch up his pants. His pants weren't really down — it was just a habit he had. It really struck me as odd, so one day I went up to him and asked him about it. "It's funny that you noticed that," he said. "I boxed for a number of years, and when you had the boxing gloves on that's the only way you could pull your trunks up."

Even though he was big and strong, he was also very gentle and very kind. He was truly a father figure to me. In the kitchen, at about 5:30 or 6:00 in the morning after feeding time, trainers or others would come up to me and ask, "Is your father here yet?" That's how close we had become and how much he had taken to me. Here's an example. The grooms used to get up at 4:30 in the morning to feed the horses. After that, I would go back to bed in my tack room for an hour or an hour and a half because our morning shift wouldn't begin until then. Duke asked me, "Sandy, where were you? I didn't see you in the kitchen." I'd explain that we'd fed at 4:30 and then I'd gone back to bed. He said, "It would be nice if I saw you down at the kitchen and have a glass of juice or something with you before we started morning workouts."

So, from that point forward, I'd feed at 4:30 and meet Duke Campbell in the kitchen at 5:30 to have some juice or a bit of breakfast. Normally, it was just the two of us, while the odd time there would be some of the other stablehands. He just wanted people to know I was a hard worker who got up early, that I was around and willing to work.

Some of the fondest memories of my whole life are from those early days at the track. True, I was living in a tack room, and in retrospect it was kind of a rough place, but we had so much fun. There were a bunch of us who worked for Duke, and we were known as Campbell's Cowboys because we *were* like a bunch of cowboys. We used to have water fights and play football up on the turf course, and I think the security guards had to visit our barn more than any other barn at the whole racetrack. Jim Mullins, who was one of Duke's best exercise riders, and I used to have wrestling matches almost every morning after galloping horses. Duke happened by one day and said, "It doesn't look like I'm working you guys hard enough." That would break up the bouts right away.

After about six months, Duke Campbell said that, if I wanted to, I could start riding some of the horses bareback around the shedrow after they had worked out, when they needed to be cooled down for thirty or forty minutes. Of course, he put me on the ones that were fairly calm. The point was for me to learn to get my balance on a horse. I was a little bit afraid to be on a horse at that point, but I got the hang of it fairly quickly.

* * *

Around this time, I had to make a decision. Duke Campbell felt I had a shot at becoming a jockey, and told me it was something I should work towards full time. My parents had no doubt that I'd be in good hands, because after meeting Duke they knew he was a wonderful man. But they were really worried, of course, about my schooling — I'd only finished Grade 10. They considered hiring a tutor, but that would have been expensive. We talked it over, and I promised that if things didn't work out I'd go back to school. They went along with that because they knew racing was something I wanted to do, and I was the right size. If, for instance, my hands or feet had been too big and it appeared as though I might have a growth spurt — and therefore not make it as a jockey — I don't think I would have pursued my career.

My parents understood that I had a chance to do exactly what I wanted to do, so they gave me the opportunity to do it. I was making a salary with Duke Campbell, so they put a nice down payment on a new car for me so that I could get around on my own. It was an Acadian — manufactured in Oshawa by Chevrolet, as it turned out. We'd looked at a variety of used cars, but a new Acadian didn't cost that much more because it was a smaller car. I lived at the racetrack, in a tack room, and this would enable me to drive home occasionally on weekends to visit. My parents wanted me to learn to respect money, so it would be up to me to keep up the payments and pay for the insurance.

I had never been away from home before, so at first life around the track was very intimidating. I was sharing a tack room with one guy, and I was looking forward to him coming home, but he had a girlfriend so he stayed at her place overnight. That left me all by myself. I had some Milk Duds or Ju-Jubes, and I lived on those for the first day because I didn't know where the kitchen was. I'd heard there was a kitchen, but I was so shy and intimidated that I didn't even eat dinner that first night. Of course, by breakfast the next day I was pretty hungry, so I followed some of the guys down to the kitchen and found out where it was.

Most of the stablehands lived in tack rooms, which were adjacent to the stalls and contained equipment, feed and things of that sort. Gordie Colbourne, who is still training horses at Woodbine today, started for Duke the same year that I did and he ended up becoming the foreman. My best friend at the racetrack at that time was Louis Hutchison. I was grooming horses and riding a horse bareback around the shedrow one day when I noticed this young guy walking around, asking where Duke Campbell was. I pointed to the tack room where the feed was stored. He went around the shedrow again and Duke later emerged to tell us the newcomer would be working for him. He asked if anybody had any available sleeping space in a tack room. I was in a room by myself at that point, and Louis and I ended up becoming best friends for a number of years. He stayed with me for a few years as I moved up the ladder, becoming a jockey and moving from the racetrack to a hotel, then an apartment, and finally a house.

I learned to ride that winter, when we returned to the National Stud Farm after the racing season ended. I started getting up on yearlings and breaking them to saddle. I was thrown off my share of times, but that was a good way to learn to ride.

The following spring, when we went back to Woodbine, I started galloping horses, and Duke told me to carry a whip all the time. It was really fantastic of Mr. Campbell to have me do that. It wasn't that I was going to go out there and use the whip right away; it was just a matter of getting used to carrying it all the time. It reached the point where it would almost feel like something was missing if I didn't have a whip in my hand. I used to climb on top of a bale of straw, pretend that it was a horse and whip it so that I'd learn the proper way to hit a horse. Duke also told me that I should practise doing with my left hand all the things I normally did with my right — from eating breakfast and dinner to brushing my teeth and combing my hair. Over the course of the year, I became practically ambidextrous.

One of the first horses I exercised provided a moment I'll never forget. It happened on the training track, which was located in the backstretch where horsemen could exercise their horses away from the hustle and bustle of the main track. Mr. Campbell told me to take the horse once around the track, which was a mile in circumference, then pull him up and bring him back to the barn. I went once around, but couldn't pull up the horse, and ended up going around another time and then a third. During the third lap, Duke — sitting on his pony, Henry — was having a good laugh. "I thought you were on the wrestling team!" he hollered. The outrider, Bob Bertrand, who is now the clerk of scales in the jockeys' room at Woodbine, came out to help me by corralling my horse. From that point on I knew you couldn't handle horses with brute strength; you had to outsmart them.

CHAPTER TWO

In the Beginning

By the spring of 1968, I had impressed Duke Campbell enough with my galloping and exercising of the horses that he was satisfied I was ready to begin my riding career. I couldn't wait to begin riding. I used to pony horses a lot for Avelino Gomez and Brian Swatuk, who both rode a lot for Duke, and watching those two great jockeys made me excited about starting my own career. There were many times when I told Duke, "I think I'm ready to start riding," but he would always reply, "*I'll* know when you're ready to start riding. You're not ready yet. I want you to really be ready before you ride your first race."

An incident at Greenwood Racetrack, after I'd been galloping horses for about a year, convinced him I was ready. Duke had a horse called Morning Rounds, and he wanted me to take him around for a mile and then pull him up. Morning Rounds was such a strong horse that no one could gallop him in the morning — no one could control him anymore. It got to the point that we put a new kind of bit on him, called draw reins, which came down and hooked up to the girth. It had an effect similar to a pulley, forcing his head down, giving me control of the horse so that I could gallop him. But one morning the girth broke and the saddle became loose and started falling. I had to kick my feet out of the stirrups, grab the saddle and gather up all the reins. I had the reins in one hand, the saddle under my arm and a handful of mane and was riding bareback. I had my balance, but Morning Rounds was out of control. He was on the outside fence, going as fast as he could, and Duke Campbell, being the horseman that he was, came out onto the racetrack, grabbed the horse by the bridle, and stopped him. He looked over at me and said, "Good, you didn't fall off. You didn't even drop the reins and didn't drop the saddle. I think you're ready to start riding races."

Before I could actually ride, the procedure at the time required me to enter into a contract with a trainer and/or owner. The contract bound the rider to the trainer or owner if they entered a horse in a race; otherwise the jockey could ride for whomever he wanted if he had an opportunity. The contract paid a stipend of $100 a month the first year, $200 the second year and $300 the third year, but in return the jockey had to ride the horses of the contracted owner or trainer for free, forfeiting any purse winnings. A jockey received $25 per mount, which would be doubled for a win, while second place would be worth $40 and third place $30. And for stakes races, the highest level of race on a card, the jockey would receive 10 percent of the purse.

Mr. Campbell offered my contract to two clients who weren't interested, but a third, Tom Hays, took him up on the offer. He had been an Alberta cattle auctioneer who had shifted his operation to the Oakville-Trafalgar area, about a twenty-minute drive west of Woodbine.

My first mount came at Woodbine on September 9, 1968, aboard a three-year-old filly called Regal Victory. She was entered in a one-mile race on the grass with a claiming tag of $2,500, which meant that she could be purchased or claimed for that fee in advance of the race by any owner or trainer — you didn't necessarily have to have a horse in the race to claim another. Claiming races make up the bulk of the races on a card, followed by allowance races and stakes. As stakes races are at the top of the scale in terms of prestige, claiming races are at the bottom. And at that time, the $2,500 level represented the bottom claimers. Regal Victory, who was owned by the partnership of J.D. Harvie and R.R. McDaniel, had run a total of thirteen times, with two wins and two third-place finishes for total earnings of $2,840. She had won her last race, running seven furlongs (or seven-eighths of a mile) with Brian Swatuk aboard. This was to be her tenth start of the season, but only her second time on the turf.

Regal Victory went to the post as the longest shot in the field of seven — at odds of more than 53–1. By comparison, the odds on the second-longest shot in the race were slightly more than 15–1. Swatuk was aboard the 6–5 post-time favourite, Chance Encounter, a five-year-old mare who had run her last seven races on the grass and had won two of them. She had come in third in her last race, in a claiming class two levels higher. Brian had ridden her in each of her turf wins and was now back aboard after a one-race absence.

Of course I was nervous, and my adrenaline was pumping before this first race. I went to the starting gate a number of times that morning. But Duke had me primed and prepped and ready to go. It was to my advantage that the race was on the turf course; it's a little more comfortable for a rider because you don't have all that dirt flying back in your face from the lead horses.

I wasn't allowed to carry a whip, because jockeys are not allowed to use one for their first five races. The stewards want to be sure that you can steer your horse straight and ride a good race. When you use a whip, you don't have as much control over the reins. I think this is a good policy; not only does it force you to develop your skills properly, but it makes matters safer for the other jockeys. It's like when you first learn to drive and you're taught to keep both hands on the steering wheel for control.

Brian Swatuk, who was the top-winning apprentice in the country the year before and who rode a lot for Duke Campbell, gave me some important advice when I started out: "When you go out there, just pretend you're as good as anybody else. Don't be intimidated at all." I remembered that for the rest of my career.

I broke okay with Regal Victory and trailed the early pacesetter, My Boy Richard, by only a length and a bit over the first quarter mile and by three lengths after half a mile, but she couldn't keep up and had dropped back to fourth at the three-quarter pole. Under Robin Platts, Nooration, the second favourite in the race at 5–2, took the lead heading into the stretch and won by two and a half lengths. I finished fifth by a little more than four and a half lengths.

When I got off the horse, my knees almost buckled. I'd been getting up on ten or twelve horses every morning for Duke Campbell and I was in really good shape, but that experience is nothing like riding in a race. It would be like a hockey player practising and then going out for a game — you can practise all you want, but there's nothing like game shape. It's the same for a rider: the actual races require you to exert yourself more, both mentally and physically, leaving you tired and sore. That first race made me realize you've got to be in a lot better shape to ride in races.

Apprentice riders are given a weight allowance to encourage trainers to use them. In horse racing, the theory is that if two horses are equal in talent, the one carrying less weight has a better chance to win, so the less weight the better. At the time I started out, an apprentice rider received a ten-pound weight break until he'd won five races; at that point it was reduced to five pounds until he graduated to the journeyman level. This promotion was determined by a number of wins and/or a period of time of a year or so.

Lou Cavalaris:
He was a natural lightweight, that didn't hurt him a damn bit. He was fearless and he had hands. It's kind of a gift, a natural gift. He wasn't that great of an exercise rider in the morning, but in the afternoon (racing), he was the man. They ran for him. And being a natural lightweight who would never have to reduce is a big, big advantage.

I count myself very fortunate that weight was never an issue for me. I stood five-foot-two and weighed about 100 pounds. (It was the same when I was on the high-school wrestling team. Fully clothed, I only weighed about 94 pounds. I'd watch others, jogging around in their warmup suits, trying to shave off that little bit of extra weight to get to 98.) But I'd guess that at least 80 percent of the guys in the jocks' room have a weight problem — some more serious than others. A lot of the guys had to go into the "hot box" to sweat off a few pounds every single day they had to ride. I can only imagine what kind of a toll that would take on you, physically and mentally.

Around the time that I was starting out, I can think of some riders who either had to watch or battle their weight. Brian Swatuk didn't have a huge weight problem, but he did have to watch it and had to hit the box once in a while. Guys like Robin Platts, Richard Grubb, Hugo Dittfach and Lloyd Duffy routinely had to go into the hot box or use other methods — such as throwing up, or what's known as "flipping" — to control their weight.

The only time I had to be concerned about my weight came after my first season of racing, when I still had the ten-pound allowance because I hadn't won five races yet. Over the course of the season I'd gotten up to 105 or 106 pounds, so at home that winter I went on a steak-and-salad diet. If I'd had access to a sweat box, I probably would have gone that route, but it was winter. Well, not only did I keep the weight off, but I actually lost a couple of pounds: when I returned to riding I was down to 104. It was a bit of a reminder that I couldn't have too much chocolate, couldn't eat ice cream or any fattening foods. And it was just a small taste of what it must be like for those who always have to worry about their weight.

Occasionally, I'd joke around in the jockeys' room by bringing a Fudgsicle into the hot box if somebody had played a prank on me. And while the prankster was trying to sweat off weight, I'd make a big deal about how hot it was in there. We joked around with one another that way a lot. In the jockeys' room, there was a lot of camaraderie. You'd be in the shower and you'd have a thing going with another rider where you'd throw a bucket of cold water on him or, as I mentioned, take a Fudgsicle into the hot box and kind of play up how hot it was in there. When we're out on the racetrack, it's every man for himself, because racing is your livelihood and no one's going to pay your bills but yourself. But that would all be put aside in the jockeys' room. It's one of the things I miss now that I'm retired. I still visit once in a while, but of course it's not the same.

I won for the first time in the sixth race of my career. It came on a two-year-old gelding called Fly Alone, which was owned by Tom Hays and trained by Duke Campbell. The horse had run twice before, finishing second in his last race, a six-furlong dash for maidens (horses that haven't won a race) with a $3,500 claiming tag. Two-year-olds are still developing physically and mentally; Fly Alone had advanced from his first start, in which he trailed the field of nine throughout a four-and-a-half-furlong race back in May at Fort Erie. That second race, in which he placed, was almost five months later, and the third start came eleven days after that, on October 14, 1968. I'll always remember it. It was a Saturday afternoon and there was a huge crowd of 14,835, almost three times the size of a midweek card.

There were eleven horses in the race, and Fly Alone went to the post as the third choice at exactly 4–1, behind a first-time starter, Nail Tip, who was the favourite at slightly more than 2–1, and Sir David at just under 7–2. Sir David's rider was John Bell, who in later years became a prominent jockey agent in Canada. Fly Alone broke well and assumed the lead soon into the race, leading at every call point and winning by four and a half lengths. That's a comfortable margin for a rider, and Fly Alone made it easy for me. It was something I'll never forget as long as I live, and it was that much more special that it happened on a horse trained by Duke Campbell.

Winning your first race is every bit as exhilarating as winning one of the big stakes races like the Queen's Plate or the Canadian Oaks. It was unbelievable. And so is what happens when you return to the jockeys' room after winning your first race. First of all, the riders showered me with buckets of ice and cold water; then came the blackballing. No, it's not like getting kicked out of a fraternity or a club; if anything, it's actually a way of being welcomed into the ranks of the jockeys. What happens is that the older riders literally paint your private parts with black dye. It's one of those old traditions that survives to this day. In my case, some of the other jockeys grabbed me and put me on a table. I didn't actually struggle too much — you put up a bit of a fight at first, but you soon realize that everybody's got a hold of you and you have no chance, so you just let them go to it and then hit the shower to try to wash off as much as you can. Of course, it takes a couple of weeks for the dye to wear off. Believe it or not, it's a wonderful feeling — a feeling of accomplishment, that is. I actually got blackballed again, after winning the Manitoba Derby in 1975 with L'Enjoleur. "Wait a minute," I said. "I'm not an apprentice." "That's too bad," they replied. "You've just won your first stakes in Winnipeg, so you're getting blackballed again." When I won my 6,000th race, I got blackballed again. It's funny when I think about it.

One of the toughest things I encountered as a young rider was switching the whip from my left hand to my right and back again. If you have a horse that is drifting in and giving you a hard time, you have to switch your whip from your right hand to your left and give your horse a slap on that side. Part of what made this so difficult for me was the fear of dropping the whip, so I got into the habit of putting the stick in my mouth and grabbing it with my left hand, just like my idol, Avelino Gomez, did. The funny thing is, I had no problem switching hands the other way, from left to right. Later in my career, when I went to California, I saw Bill Shoemaker, another jockey I idolized, and I asked him if I should try to break this habit. He replied, "You know what? You've had a lot of success with what you're doing, so I wouldn't change a thing." And I never did. You can bet that, had he advised me to, I would have changed my style.

I won my fourth career race in my thirty-eighth mount in that first season. Even though there were several racing cards left in the season, Duke Campbell had already decided to save my apprentice "bug" to maximize my apprentice period for the full 1969 Canadian season, beginning the following spring at Greenwood. The "bug" is the racing term for the apprentice's allowance, and it's called that because the mark in the official program used to designate the weight break looks like a bug. I had a mount scheduled for the last day of the 1968 Canadian meet, and Duke took me off it in case I won; the moment I won my fifth race, my weight allowance would shrink from ten pounds to five, and my apprenticeship would be activated henceforth for one year or forty victories, whichever came last. The horse that I was scheduled to ride was a bit of longshot, but Duke still didn't want to take that risk.

The following season I was hooked up with a jockey agent, Colin Wick. Duke had tried to partner me with Colin when I first started out, but Colin was booking mounts for journeyman Jim Fitzsimmons and apprentice Brian Swatuk, who was battling Robin Platts for the title of winningest rider in Canada. Colin promised Duke that if someone else took care of booking my mounts for the last part of the 1968 season, he would take over at the beginning of 1969. Colin also continued to book mounts for Brian, who had edged out Platts as the leading rider of 1968. Near the end of the year, Robin was suspended for ten days after hitting another rider on the back with his whip, and Brian came out ahead by six wins. Brian had lost his bug, but he still did well as a journeyman. Unfortunately, he suffered some injuries in 1969, including a broken collarbone at the Woodbine meet.

I was young and inexperienced at the racetrack, so I didn't know a lot about agenting and what was involved. Nor did I realize when I first met Colin how good of an agent he was. He had been a rider in his native England, but his career was cut short by injuries, including a severe one to his knee that he suffered in a morning workout mishap. In 1955 he began his career as an agent, representing his younger brother Alex, who rode for ten years and won numerous stakes races. Alex later became an agent, too, and had great success with Richard Dos Ramos.

I had seen Colin around the barn a number of times booking mounts for Brian Swatuk, and Colin was one of the best, if not *the* best, agents, not only in Canada but in all of North America. People loved to have him around — he was, and still is, a lively character. When I first met him, he took me under his wing, as Duke Campbell had done, and I was made to feel like part of his family. His wife, Margaret, was wonderful to me. Colin had a son, also named Colin, and we were about the same age. I remember going fishing with them both every once in a while.

Duke had such high hopes for me going into the 1969 season that he invited Jim Coleman, one of the deans of Canadian racetrack journalism, to sit beside him across from the finish line on opening day to watch me ride. "I'm going to let you watch a great, young rider," he said. "Maybe he's going to be the best rider you've ever seen."

Colin certainly didn't have that feeling at that time.

Colin Wick:
In the beginning, he looked just like any rider. Nobody knows how good a rider will be — I don't care who it is. You can't tell anything about a young rider coming up after only a few rides. It just developed that way.

I didn't disappoint Duke: I won my fifth career race that day with a horse called Lauren Gail. As I've mentioned, this was a significant milestone because, according to the Ontario Racing Commission's rules at the time, I now had only a five-pound weight allowance, and I would lose this in exactly one year.

Early in the season, I was aboard an odds-on favourite, Morning Rounds — the same horse who had been so hard to gallop and who had been instrumental in convincing Duke Campbell to let me begin my riding career. Morning Rounds was undefeated going into this race, but we lost after getting off to a bad start. That prompted a horseman standing next to Colin Wick to remark, "If you can make this one into a rider, you've got to be Houdini."

The owners of Morning Rounds had some twenty horses with Duke Campbell, and they told him after that experience that they didn't want me riding their horses anymore. Mr. Campbell wouldn't hear of it. "Sandy's going to be a good rider one of these days and you're going to be begging me to use him," he replied. "If you don't want Sandy riding these horses, you can take them out of my barn because I don't want to train them." The owners ended up leaving me on their horses. I always appreciated that show of support and will always remember it.

A couple of days after my twentieth birthday, an article appeared in the *Daily Racing Form* — the newspaper that is essential reading for bettors because it includes data about the past performances of the horses racing at various tracks, plus stories about horsemen and the industry. The story, written by Wally Wood, who covered the Ontario racing circuit, was headlined "Sandy Hawley a Comer," and it chronicled some of my early-season success and how I came to be a jockey. It was my first big article in the *Form*.

This quiet, serious, young man from Oshawa doesn't have the colour and the glamour of Avelino Gomez and he doesn't have the boyish appeal of Richard Grubb. What makes him attractive to the grandstand crowd could simply be his dedication in riding each race to win. "He always gives you a shot," said one supporter. In other words, the fans recognize that he gives of his best and makes the horses do likewise.

Partway through that year, Lloyd Duffy, to whom I was second in apprentice wins, lost his bug. But that didn't mean my task would be any easier: there was another notable apprentice at the time, Rudy Turcotte, who was a very good rider in his own right, and at the same time he had the Turcotte name going for him. His brothers — first Ron and later Noel — had already been successful. I didn't think there was a chance of beating Rudy. But business really started to pick up for me after Lloyd lost the bug, and that paved the way for me to win my first title: in the Fort Erie summer meet, with 39 wins from 172 mounts. Robin Platts was second with 26 wins in 158 mounts, and Hugo Dittfach was third with 22 in 185.

On August 16, 1969, I won my first career stakes race when I booted home Miss Suzaki, owned by Fred Trimble and trained by Doug Davis Jr., in the Belle Mahone for fillies and mares. I must point out that, even though I was the winning rider, it really was a team effort — and by that I mean my agent and I. Whenever I talked to reporters, I always referred to "us" or "we." This is in no way because I'm pretentious; in fact, the opposite is true. I find it hard to speak about my career and achievements in the first person because so many people have contributed to my success. And when it came to winning races, my agents played key roles — after all, they were getting me the mounts that gave me so many chances to win.

I had ridden Miss Suzaki twice before in allowance races. On one occasion, she finished last by fifteen lengths after going to the post as the 9–5 favourite in a six-horse field. She was up fairly close to the pace in the beginning of the mile-and-an-eighth race on the dirt, but couldn't keep up afterward. This time, she trailed the field again, but only by about five and a half lengths after half a mile, and she started to kick into gear when I called on her with about three-eighths of a mile to go. In the closing strides she wore down Sailor Take Care — the betting favourite in the race with her tough stablemate, Not Too Shy — to win by a neck. Miss Suzaki paid off handsomely, too, with a mutuel price of $19.60 for a $2 win ticket.

Maybe it was meant to be, considering that Wally Wood had a story in the *Daily Racing Form* that day about Duke Campbell. The story, headlined "Everyone Knows Him as Duke," chronicled Mr. Campbell's history and the origin of his nickname. It was originally Dude, which was given to him during his boxing days, but it later became Duke when he was called that by the trainer Jim Speers. Mr. Campbell worked for Speers for twenty-three years and considered him a father figure. Mr. Campbell paid me a compliment in the story when he remarked that I could be "as good a race rider as has come up in a long time. He's conscientious and always trying. And he has the ambition to be a great rider."

Things certainly worked out well in the Belle Mahone!

Des Hawley:
A lot of people said he was just a natural, that his abilities were almost born in him. It was more or less a surprise for my wife and me, but when you saw him ride he was watching and learning from the good riders that were riding at that time — Avelino Gomez, Chris Rogers. He got a lot of information from Chris Rogers, who was an excellent rider.

Veteran horse racing analyst Jim Bannon, who began working at the track as a stablehand for trainer Lou Cavalaris at about the same time I started out my career and with whom I developed a strong friendship, has his own thoughts about how I was able to succeed.

Jim Bannon:
One of Sandy's best attributes as a rider was his outstanding athleticism. He could get into a sustained

rhythm aboard his mount, especially in the late furlongs, and make the horse duplicate the cadence. They would come through the stretch as if one entity, recoiling and then extending simultaneously. Such synergy was highly effective.

In September, another story about me appeared in the *Daily Racing Form*, under the headline "Hawley — Another Shoemaker?" What a thrill it was to be compared to one of my idols. The article was written by Hot Walker — the pen name of Bruce Walker, the publicity manager of the Ontario Jockey Club. Bruce would become one of my closest and dearest friends. In his article, Bruce quoted the trainer Juan D. Agostino, who, upon watching me work one of Duke's horses, remarked: "I don't know who has that boy, but I'd sure like to have his contract. He's the best bug boy I've seen since Willie Shoemaker." Bruce wrote: "Another Shoemaker? That remains to be seen. But Sandy Hawley is almost assured of a bright and prosperous future." He also quoted Richard Grubb, the leading apprentice in 1967, who said: "I thought this spring that he was the best of all the bug boys. He's going to be tough without the bug, too."

If you're the leading apprentice rider, there's a good chance that things will work out well for you when you become a journeyman. Colin and I had set a goal for me to become the leading apprentice, and it worked out well after Lloyd lost his bug and then Rudy Turcotte left before the season's end to join his older brother, Ron, in New York. In the Woodbine meet, I had 81 winners in 44 days — again, it wasn't just me, it was "we," as in Colin and me — including a stakes victory aboard Moonreindeer, owned by Peter Fuller and trained by Jerry Meyer, in the Autumn Handicap. I finished a length in front of James Bay, who was ridden by Chris Rogers. Chris had finished second to me in the Belle Mahone Stakes back in August.

I had ridden Moonreindeer once before. Overall, he had only two wins in twenty races. Similar to the Belle Mahone, I won from off the pace. In fact, at the halfway point of the mile-and-a-quarter race, I was eleven and a half lengths back. But, heading into the stretch, I was only four lengths back of James

Bay, who had seized the lead from heavy (6–5) favourite Bye and Near. Moonreindeer headed James Bay in the last sixteenth of a mile to the wire and won by a length, his first victory in his last twelve races. He paid $10.10 to win. On that card, I had five winners in eight mounts.

Colin and I continued our torrid streak in the Greenwood fall meet, with 76 wins in 224 mounts. Overall, I finished as the leading rider in the nation, with 230 wins from 920 mounts. I also had 151 seconds and 123 thirds for an in-the-money average of more than 50 percent. I averaged almost two winners a day and posted three or more victories on more than twenty cards. (I also had four five-day riding suspensions, but that's part of the learning curve for most young riders.) Overall, my mounts earned $615,078, which was about a quarter of the earnings of the top money-winning jockey in North America in 1969, Jorge Velasquez.

I went out with my parents and bought a new car, a Chevy Impala, unbeknownst to Duke and Colin. The Impala was a huge car with three big tail lights on either side at the back. I'll never forget it. When I brought it home, my folks said, "You know what? Maybe this car is too big for you right now. If you go driving this to the racetrack, they're going to think success has gone to your head." At the time, my dad was driving a Chevy Malibu, which was smaller and about a year old. I suggested that we switch for a year, at which point we'd trade. And that's exactly what we did. And I did feel much more comfortable driving to the track in "my" year-old car, knowing that no one could accuse me of getting a swelled head.

After the 1969 season, the plan was for me to go to Florida to exercise horses for Frank Merrill, one of the top trainers in Ontario, who regularly had a string down south in the winter and did quite well. It turned out to be a memorable time in more ways than one. Duke, Colin and I drove Tom Hays' car to Florida, and a funny thing happened crossing the border into the U.S. at Fort Erie. Tom had packed a portion of his trunk with freeze-dried meat — he planned to stock his freezer at his Florida home — and hadn't told us about it. At the border crossing, we were asked if we had anything to declare, and we replied that we hadn't. All of a sudden they were looking in the trunk and finding the meat. You're not supposed to take meat across the border, and there we were, smuggling some. They went through all our bags, and Colin was pretty nervous about it — he even thought we might go to jail. I was only nineteen at the time, and I was pretty scared myself. One of the customs agents recognized Duke, and then me, and gave us a break. They ended up confiscating the meat, but otherwise we were allowed to go through without incident.

My plan to gallop horses changed when the Ontario Racing Commission altered its rules for apprentice riders, removing a concession that allowed them to carry over their bug to the following Canadian season if it was not used in winter racing in the U.S. Therefore, I started riding regularly at Tropical Park in Miami, winning on my debut on December 30 and finishing the meet with 19 wins, 18 seconds and 15 thirds from 110 mounts. Then I shifted to Hialeah and became the first apprentice to win the meet, beating the likes of such veterans as Braulio Baeza, Angel Cordero Jr., Eddie Belmonte, Jacinto Vasquez, Charles Baltazar, Bill Hartack, Earlie Fires and Michael Hole. It was the thrill of a lifetime — these guys were like movie stars to me.

I was riding a lot of horses for Arnold Winick, who had one of the top outfits in the U.S. and who used to battle it out with Frank Merrill. Colin couldn't act as my agent in the States because he didn't have his working papers, so I was represented by a gentleman named Sandy Arden. Was he ever a character! He could have played gangsters in the movies — he had that raspy, New York tough guy kind of voice. And to describe him as a character in these surroundings was saying something: Belmonte, Cordero and Jorge Velasquez always used to dress to the nines in these very colourful suits — in blue, pink, mauve, purple — and with the hats to match. It was like a film set.

Two weeks into the Hialeah meet, things were going well for my agent and me. We'd had fourteen winners, and that caught the eye of *Daily Racing Form* writer Joe Hirsch, who in later years became the dean of racing writers and whom, in the 1980s, I asked to formally introduce me when I was inducted into the National Museum of Racing Hall of Fame.

"For the first time in memory, one jockey rode three winners on the grass in one afternoon here, and each of Hawley's efforts was a jewel," Joe Hirsch wrote. "The 20-year-old has poise beyond his experience. He is not afraid to wait with a horse, in sharp contrast to the go-go tactics of most young jockeys, and that is why an apprentice is the leading rider of the meeting, competing against the Baezas, the Hartacks, the Velasquezes, the Vasquezes, the Corderos, the Rotzes and the others."

The Hialeah meet ended on March 3, and we won it with 42 wins, seven ahead of Jacinto Vasquez. But this success complicated matters. The Ontario racing season was to start on March 26, 1970, at Greenwood, but this conflicted with the season in Florida, which shifted to Gulfstream Park after the close of the Hialeah meet and continued until April 22. Tom Hays had been my manager and wanted to stay in Florida and maintain my business down there, especially with Arnold Winick, who had a three-year-old colt on the Kentucky Derby trail, Corn off the Cob, whom I had ridden to victory in a prep race for the Flamingo Stakes. I had also ridden Dust Commander, another top Derby horse. The thing was, I was homesick; my mother had had come to visit me a few times to keep me company.

Mr. Hays said I would definitely miss the Ontario season opener, but could possibly return for Sunday racing during downtime at Gulfstream. Duke Campbell, who co-owned my contract, told The Globe and Mail's Lou Cauz that he thought it would be good for me to stay in Florida, if only because I stood to make more money in a considerably shorter time. In almost two months in Florida, I'd earned almost as much as I had in all of the previous season.

Duke told Lou that he had received several inquiries from people wanting to purchase the contract. Lou reported on rumours that Winick was offering between thirty and fifty thousand dollars for the right to use my services on a first-call basis. Mr. Campbell wouldn't confirm the figures, but he said it would be "awfully hard" to turn down the offer he'd been made. A few weeks later, he sold his interest in the contract to Tom Hays for an undisclosed price.

Immigration problems forced me to return home in April to get my working papers straightened out — not an uncommon occurrence at the time for a Canadian rider. I left Gulfstream Park having ridden 37 winners, far more than anyone else, gathered up my tack and headed to Fort Erie for the spring meet. I won with four of my seven mounts on opening day.

Bob Pennington, the racing writer for the *Toronto Telegram*, wrote an article about me in which he quoted Duke Campbell as saying: "Last season we knew he was good. Now we know he's great. Riding in Florida has given him that extra polish, that touch of confidence. The result is class." To Duke's comments, Bob Pennington added his own: "Sandy Hawley is to racing what Bobby Hull is to hockey — the best image constructor in the business. Hull, to his credit, works at it. With Hawley it is a case of simply being Sandy Hawley."

The Fort Erie meet ended and I finished on top with 21 wins, two ahead of Lloyd Duffy and three more than Dick Armstrong. Now it was on to Woodbine, where I would get my first taste of success in the major Canadian races, beginning with the Canadian Oaks, the most important race for three-year-old Canadian-bred fillies. Beginning in 1970, I would win the Oaks five times in a row. The first of these was aboard Charles Taylor's South Ocean, who upset the favourite, Fanfreluche. Fanfreluche was the reigning Canadian horse of the year, and in her first four starts this year had racked up two wins, a second and a third. South Ocean, meanwhile, had been winless in her first three starts of the season after winning three of ten the year before. She was a daughter of New Providence, who had won the Canadian Triple Crown in 1959, which meant she had the stamina on her sire's side to cover the Oaks' distance of a mile and an eighth on the dirt. In her last meeting with Fanfreluche, she'd placed second by a length.

Fanfreluche went postward at less than even money, while my filly was backed at slightly more than 4–1 odds. I had South Ocean far back for three-quarters of a mile, then I asked her to run; she circled the field, rallied on the far turn and overtook Fanfreluche, who set the pace, in the final eighth of a mile. She won by two and a half lengths. It was just a tremendous thrill to be in the winner's circle at the Canadian Oaks for Mr. Taylor. South Ocean went on to become a prolific broodmare, producing the multiple Canadian champion Northernette and the 1980 English/Irish champion, Storm Bird.

As the Queen's Plate loomed closer, I began to look forward to my first ride in the historic race. Open only to Canadian-bred three-year-olds, the Plate is the pinnacle of Canadian horse racing — it's Canada's equivalent to the Kentucky Derby. I had my choice of three or four mounts, and after talking to Colin Wick we settled on Malcolm Smith's Almoner, a compact bay gelding I had ridden two starts before. In that race, we'd finished second by half a length to the highly rated Two Violins. Trained by Lou Cavalaris for George Gardiner, Two Violins won all five of his starts as a three-year-old, and would have been the Plate favourite except that he injured a leg while training for the race.

In his last race, a division of the Plate Trial Stakes, Almoner finished second while being ridden by John LeBlanc. John had the misfortune of having his saddle slip on him and he lost considerable ground, but rallied hard to place by only a head. Almoner gave every indication that he would appreciate the extra eighth of a mile of the Plate's mile-and-a-quarter distance. His sire, Victoria Park, had won the Plate in 1960, the year he finished third in the Derby and second in the Preakness, the first two legs of the American Triple Crown. His winning time of two minutes and two seconds in the Plate had been the fastest since the race had been lengthened from a mile and an eighth in 1957.

Speaking as a jockey, it was tough to arrive at the decision to ride Almoner; I had ridden most of the other contenders before, and sometimes when you're riding good horses you can't tell which one is the best if they haven't raced one another. For me, taking Almoner was kind of like flipping a coin. As my agent, Colin made most of the calls about whom we were going to ride. As it turned out, we ended up making the right call, because Almoner ended up running a big race.

Riding in the Queen's Plate for the first time was nerve-racking. I was more nervous going into that race than for any other in my career, except perhaps for my first mount ever. The

Queen's Plate is so prestigious, and if that weren't enough, I was on one of the favourites. You feel the pressure even more when you're riding one of the favourites because you're naturally expected to finish in the money — if not win the race — so you don't want to make any mistakes.

Dance to Market, the champion Canadian two-year-old colt or gelding in 1969, had been made the race favourite at 5–2; he was to be ridden by Chris Rogers, who had won the Plate three times. By post time, Almoner had become the betting favourite at just under 3–1, while Dance to Market went postward at slightly more than 5–1. The coupled entry of Fanfreluche and Croquemitaine, both owned by Jean-Louis Levesque, was the second most popular with the bettors at almost 7–2.

Dance to Market forged to the front after half a mile and led for a while, but Fanfreluche took over at the top of the stretch. I knew Almoner was the type of horse that would sit just off the pace; I wheeled him out with three-eighths of a mile to the wire, and I felt a lot better when, with a quarter mile to go, we sat five lengths off the lead. I knew I was going to win with an eighth of a mile to go, although Fanfreluche was still running well. I think I went to the front at about the seventy-yard pole and won by three-quarters of a length. Describing Almoner's effort, the *Daily Racing Form* chart noted, "Unhurried through the first half mile, moved steadily from the outside to reach a striking position entering the stretch and, responding to energetic handling, wore down Fanfreluche in the closing yards."

I hadn't ridden in a lot of stakes races before, but Almoner stacked up well against many of the good horses I'd had the opportunity to ride to that point in my career.

After the race, trainer Jerry Lavigne and owner Malcolm Smith invited me to the Constellation Hotel for a victory celebration. I was living at the Ascot Hotel at the time, and most of my family, including aunts and uncles, were there because they wanted to watch me ride. (My mother came to the races, too, even though, after seeing me take a few spills during my first season, she couldn't bear to look until after the races were over. Once a race had ended, she would watch the replay.) We'd planned to go out for dinner as a family after the Plate, but they encouraged me to go to the victory celebration and assured me they would wait at the hotel until I returned. I ended up staying at the party until about midnight, and even though I didn't usually drink, I'd had about three or four glasses of champagne, so I was feeling pretty good by the time I got home. My dad said later that when I got home I was jumping up and down on the bed as if it was a trampoline. That's how excited I was. The next day, I was slated to ride about seven or eight mounts, and I had a pretty bad headache from the champagne. It was my first hangover ever. The horses must have sensed something was up and taken pity on me, because I think I won four races that day.

The Prince of Wales Stakes is the second leg of the Canadian Triple Crown, and it takes place at Fort Erie. In those days, the race was run on the grass, and almost three months after the Plate (today, the interval is only three weeks, and like the Queen's Plate, the Prince of Wales is run on the dirt). That gave Almoner time to run twice after the Plate. He won his first start, which was on the dirt, and came in third by three-quarters of a length in his next start, which was on the turf. Going into the Prince of Wales Stakes, I probably felt as much pressure as I had in the Plate, because I had won the first jewel in the Triple Crown. But Almoner was such a nice horse, and I think he overcame my nervousness. He was the betting favourite, at slightly more than even money, and he led almost all the way, surrendering the lead to Northern Monarch only briefly on the far turn, but regaining control and winning by a length and a half.

The Triple Crown concludes at Woodbine with the Breeders' Stakes — at a mile and a half, the longest of the three races. Unlike the Prince of Wales, the Breeders' continues to be run on the turf. That year, the Breeders' Stakes took place a month after the Prince of Wales (once again, the time between races has been compressed; these days, all three races happen in the span of about six weeks). As it stood at the time, the Triple Crown was a real test of stamina and durability — jockeys and horses alike had to keep sharp and sound from June all the way into October. Only two horses had swept all three jewels: New Providence in 1959 and Canebora in 1963. That's how it remained until 1989, when With Approval became the first of four winners in just five years. Then, after Peteski in 1993, we had to wait another decade before Wando completed the triple. Since it was created in 1959, there have been only seven winners.

There was never any doubt that we would stick with Almoner and try to win the Triple Crown. And because the chance to sweep was such a rarity, riding in the Breeders' was probably as tough on me as the previous two stakes races had been. Going in, I was afraid of Mary of Scotland, the filly trained by Lou Cavalaris and owned by Gardiner Farm. She had ran third in the Canadian Oaks, and I had won aboard her in her last race before the Breeders'.

Lou Cavalaris:
Sandy told me Mary of Scotland was the better horse going that far on the turf. Almoner was a special horse, but the turf wasn't his favourite thing and a mile and a half certainly wasn't to his liking. For Mary of Scotland, the turf was her whole ballgame, and a mile and a half was the perfect length. On the dirt, though, Almoner was a better horse.

I had Almoner well positioned, moving him up to the point where he was second by only a head with half a mile to go. But Mary of Scotland, with Richard Grubb aboard, was moving with a rush after having started off unhurried and been under strong restraint in the early part of the race. Rounding the final turn, she took control. All of a sudden I saw this big, bay mare sweeping past us, and I didn't even have to look over to know it was Mary of Scotland. She finished nine and a half lengths ahead of my horse at the finish.

Needless to say, it was very disappointing to lose the Triple Crown. Winning the Plate was the ultimate prize, but I just know that the Triple Crown would have been every bit as exciting.

It was around this time that the *Toronto Telegram*'s Mike Armstrong wrote a story about me and quoted Avelino Gomez, who had retired midway through the previous year. He was effusive in his praise:

> There's no doubt he's the king. He does everything right, just like I used to, so I make him the king like I used to be. He's two or three lengths better than the rest of the jockeys, no doubt about it. And everything is in his favour. He's young, rides live horses, has a good brain and, most important, he's a good rider. I think he learned a lot when he went away to Florida last winter. He watched those top riders and he learned. Before he left, I told him to ride the same there as he did here. I told him that I came back from there and beat them all here, and he could do the same. Look what he's doing now. He's the king for as long as he wants to be.

Avelino set a Canadian record with 304 victories in 1966, but we were drawing close to eclipsing the mark. I had a great September, winning 69 races in 214 mounts, which ranked as the most productive month in racing history by a rider racing at only one track a day. In 1965, Jesse Davidson had won 71 races in August, but he rode day and night at two separate tracks and totalled 269 mounts. In nine cards between the fifth and seventeenth of September, I posted 33 winners. Between the months of July and November, I won 273 races.

Ronnie Robinson:
I'd had a lot of riders up until that point — and some pretty good ones — but he improved so fast it just amazed me. It was hard to believe, from one month to the next, the changes he would make in his riding — the adjustments he would make in moving on horses, not moving too soon and waiting. It was unbelievable. And the desire he showed coming to the wire, it was uncanny. I used to always say, "You're nearly there. You're not as good as Gomey yet. But you're coming close." It was hard to believe that somebody could do the things that Gomez did. He did things that nobody else could accomplish, if you want to know the truth to

my way of thinking. And Sandy copied him in a lot of ways.

In the midst of this glorious period, Lou Cauz of *The Globe and Mail* wrote a story about Tom Hays' unhappiness with me. Under the headline "Has the Good Life Spoiled Sandy Hawley?", he expressed concern about my lifestyle and work ethic. He was critical of my long hair and moustache, my living quarters away from the track, my sports car and my refusal to work horses in the morning. He concluded I had become undisciplined and too big for my britches.

As far as I was concerned, I was working very hard, going to morning workouts, getting on horses for Duke Campbell and getting on horses for a lot of other people. As for the long hair and moustache, that was the style back then. Bell-bottoms were coming out, long hair was really in style, but I still brought the same work ethic anytime I rode horses for people. Sure, I looked a little different, but I still had the same personality.

Wilf Stevenson, the clerk of scales at Greenwood, was quoted in an article by the *Toronto Star*'s Frank Orr as saying that I hadn't changed since the first day I came to the track.

I was good friends with Brian Swatuk, Richard Grubb, Robin Platts and Lloyd Duffy, and we'd go down to Toronto's Yorkville district to buy our clothes. If you wanted to buy platform shoes, shoes with a heel, that's where you went — that's where they were most readily available. I remember going down there with Brian Swatuk a few times. I was good friends with Brian's brother, Barry, who was grooming and exercising horses for Duke Campbell. Barry was one of the first people I ever saw wearing bell-bottoms — and this was before they were even the fashion. I asked him once, "What the heck are you wearing?" He said, "You'll see: these things are coming in style." A year later, there I was, wearing them too. So was everyone else. Barry was a little bit ahead of his time.

I was also into loud rock music and wore Led Zeppelin T-shirts, but from where I stood, success really hadn't gone to my head.

Ronnie Robinson:
When he started out he just had T-shirts and
sweatshirts. In the second full year that he rode, he
finally bought a pair of shoes and a suit and a tie. The
standard thing with me was, "Listen, kid, you go get a
haircut and I'll work for you for the month for
nothing." He was just a kid, acting like a lot of other
kids, and he loved that rock music. Sandy could talk to
you about that music even today. He loved it.

The president of Spalding sporting goods made
him a handmade set of clubs, and Sandy was supposed
to go the factory for a presentation. He came in with a
Superman sweater. The president of Spalding said, "I
can see success hasn't gone to your head, son." He was
just a big kid, and money had no value to him.

In the beginning, people were knocking him
because of his hair and the way he rode. He had a spell
of being lazy, staying up late at night and listening to
music. A lot of people claimed he was on drugs and
drinking, but Sandy never got into any of that stuff.
People were looking to find a hole in him. That's really
what it was. He was the Boy Wonder and people would
wonder why — what's he doing that's making him so
good? I guess if you were thinking about it today,
they'd be wondering if he was using steroids or
something. But he never used drugs, and I knew he
didn't drink because I'd go out to different functions
with him and he'd have a Coke or something. It was an
oddity if he ever had a beer and he's still that way today.

He had fierceness in his riding, relentlessness. He
never showed any weakness. He'd ride the tenth horse
on the card just the same way he rode the first. And
he'd be running fifth or sixth and he'd still be driving
on a horse, aiming for fourth-place money. He never
seemed to want to give up. He was a poor man's rider
— drive for that fourth money, man, get some oat
money back.

They called him God in a respectful way. You
wouldn't believe it, but when riders used to hear or see

him coming, they'd be saying at the quarter-pole [from the wire] or the three-sixteenths pole, "Man, he's got me. I'm dead now. I know I can't beat him." I've heard riders say that. They'd come back in the jocks' room and say, "Christ, I thought I was in good shape; then I could hear him coming and I'd look over and there he is and I knew there's no way I was going to outride him to the wire."

On November 9, I became only the fourth rider in history to win 400 races in a season, putting me amongst such elite company as Bill Shoemaker, Bill Hartack and Jorge Velasquez. The next day, I booted home five winners to surpass Avelino Gomez's four-year-old Canadian record of 304 wins. Gomez was my idol when I first started, when all I wanted to do was get my name in the program of the day's races. To all of a sudden break his record was a tremendous thrill, something I'd never dreamed was possible. But I had a great agent, and things were going well.

Mayor William Dennison declared November 20 Sandy Hawley Day in Toronto and warned me to "stay away from tobacco, drugs and too much liquor." He declared me to be a "son of Toronto who has brought recognition to his city."

The Ontario Jockey Club also honoured me with a Sandy Hawley Day at Greenwood. The presentation coincided with the birthday of my eighty-year-old maternal grandmother, Mary Campbell. John J. Mooney, the managing director of the Ontario Jockey Club, praised my parents for rearing such a "fine boy and a fine rider." I had my picture taken with a number of the riders. It was unbelievable. When I'd first started galloping horses and hadn't yet begun to ride, if somebody so much as said to me, "Hey, jock, how ya doing today," it would have been enough of a thrill simply to have someone think I was a jockey.

My dad was asked by reporters about my accomplishments, and he said: "He sure makes you proud. Four years ago I would never have guessed he'd be the top jockey in North America. I wouldn't have even guessed he'd be a jockey."

One reporter asked my mom if she was proud of what I had achieved that year. She replied, "I was proud of him the day he was born."

To have my grandmother there — she was getting pretty old and I knew she didn't have a whole lot of time left — was wonderful. She'd been living with us for a number of years and we ended up becoming very close.

I finished the Ontario season with 342 winners, and 451 overall when my wins at various other racetracks were totalled up. I needed only 35 wins to break Bill Shoemaker's world record of 485 wins, set in 1953, and I was heading to Florida, where I had had so much success the year before. The record seemed within reach.

Because of the year I was having, Tom Hays seemed to be getting more actively involved. So many people were expressing interest in buying my contract, and since he was a businessman I think he saw the dollar signs. A jockey agent, Francis "Blackie" Mesite, approached Tom and told him he could get a large amount for my contract if he, Blackie, were allowed to book my mounts in Florida that winter, so he was engaged. I won a race on opening day, but I went through a dry spell immediately thereafter. After my first twenty mounts, I still only had that one winner. I didn't seem able to pick up the hot horses that had come my way so easily the year before with Sandy Arden. Many people said the problem related directly to Mesite. Frankie Merrill and Arnold Winick said they weren't going to ride me on their horses unless I changed agents because they didn't like him around their barn. They didn't consider him friendly and just didn't like to see him. I wanted to rehire Sandy Arden, and pleaded my case to the Hialeah stewards, but they couldn't do anything because Tom Hays had my contract and he was the one who had hired Mesite. So I went to Mr. Hays and told him that, since all these people didn't like Francis Mesite, I thought we ought to switch back to Arden. Hays rejected the idea, in his usual loud, boisterous manner: "I'm making the calls around here, and Francis is going to stay as your agent. I don't care what people say."

My business still didn't get any better, so I called Colin Wick in Canada and said, "You've got to come here and help me, because things aren't working out and Tom Hays won't let me change agents. Nobody likes him around the shedrow." I needed someone to talk to Tom Hays — someone who stood a better chance of being heard than I would on my own.

Colin flew all the way down to Florida to see Tom. We went to his beautiful home — I stayed at a house he had in Hallandale, near Gulfstream Park — to talk about changing agents. Tom poured Colin a drink and said, "Good to see you again." Colin immediately said, "I'm here to talk to you about Sandy and the agent he has that nobody likes." Tom replied, "If I would have known that's what you came to talk about, I wouldn't have even given you a drink."

Colin Wick:
When he told us what he was going to do with Sandy, I said, "You're not going to do nothing with him. Take this drink and stick it." Sandy didn't know anything. He was a kid. He didn't know what's going on. Years and years ago, somebody had to hold a contract for an apprentice jockey to ride. Today they don't — things have changed. When I got down there, Sandy had just quit riding. He said, "I'm not going to ride for this guy." But at that time, if you didn't ride for your contract-holder, he could keep you from riding for anybody else.

One writer noted, "A good horse can make a bad rider look good, but not even Ben Hur could make a bad horse win." Of my first 35 mounts, 29 failed to finish in the top three, while 21 were dismissed by the bettors at odds longer than 7–1. One horse went off at a whopping 109–1!

My business was really tailing off, and I didn't want to stay in Florida any longer. It was just very, very frustrating for me. Because of the bad meet, I didn't come close to breaking Shoemaker's mark. Still, I finished the year with 452 winners — the most in North America — from 1,908 mounts. And in total, I racked up $1,716,838 in purses, which placed me ninth overall on the continent. Laffit Pincay Jr., at $2,626,526, was the leading money winner.

In the new year, I retained the Toronto-based lawyer Tony Hendrie to plead my case against Tom Hays to the Tropical Park stewards. Tom threatened to send me home and exercise horses at Duke Campbell's farm in Gormley. The situation was only resolved when I gave up my fight, realizing that nothing could be done until the contract expired on June 29, 1971.

In a statement to the media, I wrote: "My interest is in my work as a professional jockey and my performance is a matter of record. I do not presently intend to take any action in the courts or to ask the Ontario Racing Commission to intervene in any difference with Tom Hays over my apprentice contract. I have been advised of my rights under the contract and otherwise, but as the contract has only a few months to run, legal proceedings would probably not be concluded prior to the termination of the contract. I am not happy about matters at present. I do not admit for a moment that Mr. Hays has the right to select my agent, and I would prefer Sandy Arden, who did a good job for me in Florida last year. However, any dispute is between me and Mr. Hays, and I think it is bad for racing to air these matters publicly. I make this statement to put matters straight, and I did not raise them."

Mr. Hays' refusal to help me drew sharp criticism from the horse racing community, but he stood by his decision and lashed back at his naysayers in an article written by *The Globe & Mail*'s Lou Cauz. Mr. Hays claimed I'd received bad advice and blamed my parents and my advisers, and suggested if I had listened to him I would have broken Shoemaker's record.

Ed Gorman, the supervisor of thoroughbred racing at the Ontario Racing Commissioner, told Cauz that Hays must have a valid reason for his actions, and said that the Florida stewards would likely stand by his actions. But he said he'd never come across a "more mannerly or proper rider" than me. He said I had always been a "perfect gentleman" and that he was sorry to see what was happening.

To appease Hays, I cut my hair a couple weeks later. I thought maybe, since he'd brought it up before, that was the problem preventing me from riding horses for some of the top trainers. Francis Mesite had given me a little package, which I thought was a gift, but it turned out to be a pair of scissors to cut my hair. I got the message: I cut my hair to please people, and hopefully to turn my business around and start riding for trainers such as Arnold Winick and Frank Merrill. But my hair wasn't the problem.

It was my agent.

CHAPTER THREE

Breaking Free

Fortunately, my difficulties with Tom Hays ended on March 23, when Art Stollery leased the remainder of my contract. A mining engineer by profession, Mr. Stollery had been making his living primarily in cattle breeding since 1956 and had been a longtime business associate of Hays'. He was a relative newcomer to the horse-racing and breeding business, which he'd been involved in for six years.

Colin Wick played a key role in the deal. He was good friends with Stollery, who approached him to find out more about the contract situation, and cleared up some uncertainties that Hays had left in his mind. Mr. Stollery bought the contract and generously agreed to pay me 10 percent of my horses' purse earnings, as well as to give Hays 10 percent of the horses' earnings. Colin told Mr. Stollery that he was doing more than he had to, but that was the way he did business: generously, and practically.

A major reason why Mr. Stollery took over the contract was because it meant locking me up to ride Kennedy Road, who had raced in the silks of Mr. Stollery's wife, Helen. I'd been aboard him for most of his nine races. He won six of them, including five in a row, but the streak came to an end when he ran a disappointing seventh in the Remsen Stakes — a major North American race for two-year-olds at Aqueduct in New York — in November. He required surgery afterwards to remove a chip from one of his ankles. Still, he was voted Canada's champion two-year-old in 1970 and was installed as the Winterbook favourite for the '71 Queen's Plate.

Mrs. Stollery had three horses on the Ontario circuit — Kennedy Road, Gallant Glen and Lauries Dancer. (I had also ridden Lauries Dancer. I was aboard her for her first career win, in fact.) Each of them had been offered for sale for

$30,000 before their first career races — that was the Stollerys' policy as breeders. That no one bought them turned out to be a stroke of good luck for the Stollerys.

I was more than happy with the the Stollerys' decision to take over the contract because of the way things had gone sour with Tom Hays and my business in Florida. I remember talking to Duke Campbell, who mentioned that Mr. Hays was thinking of passing the contract over to Art Stollery, and I said, "Gee, that's fine with me."

I had six mounts on the opening card of the 1971 Canadian season at Greenwood, and I won only one race, with a horse called Early Victory. Perhaps that was a positive omen: I had 15 winners in the first seven cards and concluded the meet with 35 winners, 13 ahead of apprentice Gary Stahlbaum. On May 2 at Fort Erie, I recorded six wins for the first time in my career. It began with Golden Bonze in the second, Royal Regina in the third, King's Champion in the fourth, Hurluburlu in the fifth, Lauries Dancer in a stakes race in the seventh and Ivy's Prince in the eighth.

Kennedy Road made his season debut about three weeks later in the Marine Stakes, a stop on the road to the Queen's Plate. Dick Armstrong had the ride in this race because I was serving a riding suspension. Kennedy Road chased Briartic all the way in the seven-furlong race, which Briartic won by two lengths in an eye-catching 1:22 3/5 after zipping through the opening six furlongs in 1:09 2/5. (That time equalled the clocking posted by Jumpin Joseph two years before, and Jumpin Joseph went on to win the Plate.) For a horse coming back from a six-month layoff, during which he had leg surgery and missed training time because of a separate illness, Kennedy Road did well. And he won his next start, eight days later. I was riding on this occasion, having served my suspension, and won a one-mile grass race by five and a half lengths.

Thirteen days later it was time for the Oaks, which drew a field of ten, although the focus was on Lauries Dancer and Painted Pony. The last time they'd met, Painted Pony — as the 3–5 favourite — had lost to my filly by a length and a half; two races before that, she'd lost by a length and a half as well. The crowd of 13,589 made Painted Pony the 3–2 favourite, followed by Lauries Dancer at slightly more than 5–2 odds, and Main Pan, who had won three of six races on the season, at 3–1. Lauries Dancer was a classy filly; she really behaved herself and was pretty easy-going in the post parade. A horse like that saves its energy for the race. With about three-eighths of a mile to go in the mile-and-one-eighth race, Painted Pony's rider, Jimmy Kelly, and I made our moves. Jimmy advanced to second, two and a half lengths behind the leader, Connie Pat, while I was fourth, about three lengths behind.

These fillies had never run a mile and an eighth before, so it was good to ride a filly that came from just a little off the pace. Soon after straightening out in the stretch, I took the lead and drew clear to win by a length and a half over Painted Pony.

It turned into a wonderful weekend for the Stollerys, trainer Jim Bentley and me when Kennedy Road made his third start of the season the next day and dominated by an eye-catching seven and a half lengths in his division of the Plate Trial Stakes. He dominated the field and won so easily that I was very confident going into the Queen's Plate. Meanwhile, Chatty Cavalier, trained by Lou Cavalaris for George Gardiner, won the first division by two lengths. In that division, I rode Mrs. Stollery's Gallant Glen, but he placed a non-threatening seventh. I had ridden Chatty Cavalier numerous times — including his last start, which he won by a length and a half — but had committed myself to Gallant Glen. Two races before the Plate Trial, I rode him and he won by five and a half lengths — beating, among others, Chatty Cavalier.

Neither Gallant Glen nor Lauries Dancer was pointed towards the Plate, which in those days was run only six days after the Plate Trial (compared with about two weeks later now). Gallant Glen was actually gelded during the week of the Plate, while Lauries Dancer wasn't even considered a candidate — the Stollerys and Jim Bentley believed that fillies should run exclusively against their own sex.

The Plate drew a field of nine, but Kennedy Road, who was clearly back in the form he had shown the previous autumn, before his injury, looked to be the solid favourite.

While I was confident about Kennedy Road's ability, I had concerns about him getting lackadaisical if he got on the lead. Sometimes he'd hang when he got on the lead and wait for his competition to come. That wasn't his only quirk. He had a temper, too, right from his two-year-old year, and as he got older he hurt some grooms in his stall. Kennedy Road was, without a doubt, the meanest, nastiest horse I ever rode in post parade in my entire career — which spanned 34,000 races. He was the worst. A guy by the name of Dave Graham used to pony him — he was an excellent pony boy, and he was able to control Kennedy Road. He'd help me on the way to the starting gate. If it weren't for Dave, I'd have been in trouble because he knew the horse and knew exactly what to do with him. Dave would actually whack him across the nose with the shank to get his attention — the colt would scream and holler and try to mount the pony all the way to the starting gate if he didn't do that.

I was riding him once at Hialeah in Florida and the pony boy wanted to grab him. That made me nervous because I didn't have Dave Graham on my side. I told the pony boy how rough and tough Kennedy Road was, but he couldn't have been prepared for what happened next. Kennedy Road just reared straight up in the air, screaming and hollering at the pony on his hind legs. The pony boy had to let him go, and when he came back down he was on the run — all I could do was scream at everyone to get out of the way. Finally, the pony boy caught up to him and we got him under control. Kennedy Road probably would have been a better horse if he didn't use so much energy going to the starting gate. He really didn't have his mind on the business at hand.

Which is not to say he wasn't a great horse — he was, and he went to California and won some major races, including the Hollywood Gold Cup. It's just that if he had been a calmer horse instead of being so skittish, I think he would have been even better than he was. I think he had a little bit more ability than he gave. When he raced, he would see another horse coming and he'd try to drift out towards him. As I said, when he took the lead, he'd wait a little bit. When he saw the competition, he'd go on, but he was the type of horse that you'd just never know what he was going to do.

The crowd of more than 30,000 bet Kennedy Road down to 9–20, the lowest odds for a Queen's Plate favourite in five years. The pressure was on because he was such a short favourite. He was still mean and nasty in the post parade, and I reserved him off the pace for the opening half mile, but I had him in full acceleration heading into the stretch, at which point he had a comfortable three-length lead. He really didn't hang that much, and he won by a comfortable three and a half lengths. He ran the mile and a quarter in 2:03, only one and one-fifth seconds off the course record and only a second behind the Plate record set by his sire, Victoria Park, in 1960.

I was happy for the Stollerys and Jim Bentley. Art Stollery was a lot of fun to be around; he loved the game and he loved life itself. He liked to have a few drinks now and then and, like my agent Colin Wick, was quite a character. Mrs. Stollery loved owning the horses; she was a wonderful, kind, soft-spoken woman. Mr. Bentley was also very kind. I loved riding for him because, when you got beat on one of his horses, he didn't really get that upset; he just wanted to know what happened. He did a masterful job of conditioning Kennedy Road back from his injury. Two-year-olds don't always maintain their form into their three-year-old year, especially after an injury, but he outdid himself this time. Mr. Bentley's double in the Oaks and Plate matched a feat by Pete McCann in 1957 with Mrs. E.P. Taylor's La Belle Rose and Lyford Cay. Horatio Luro repeated that five years later with Taylor's sensational filly Flaming Page, who won both races. Mr. Bentley, who was in his sixties at that time, had been born in Ireland but he bounced around Canadian racetracks for almost forty-five years. He galloped the 1927 Plate winner Troutlet. In 1949, he won the historic Travers Stakes — the Midsummer Derby, as it's commonly known — with Arise at Saratoga. His last Plate hopeful prior to Kennedy Road had been in 1956 with Argent, who overcame a terrible start after the starting-gate doors closed on his tail to run second to Canadian Champ.

* * *

Despite my success, I was running into a series of suspensions — that would run for five days apiece — from the stewards for riding infractions. By mid-July I had already racked up four, equalling the entire number I'd been assessed the year before. It got to the point where I'd be looking back at the tote board to see if my horse's number was flashing — indicating that the stewards were reviewing the running of the race for a possible riding infraction. I publicly stated that I might leave Ontario to ride full time in the U.S. because of the suspensions. "Wherever I go I'll learn to keep my head up or correct whatever they think I'm doing wrong here," I said. "Maybe elsewhere there won't be so many claims of foul." While I was known as a gentleman rider, I wanted to be the first one to the wire. I did just about everything I could to get there first. I was already an aggressive rider — if there wasn't already a hole there, I'd make one.

Chris McCarron once said, "If a horse responds from the whip, shame on him." There were some horses you'd hit with the whip and they'd respond; then again, there were others who wouldn't really respond, so I wouldn't hit them very much. If I hit the horse and he responded and was going to get to the wire easily, I wasn't about to hit him very much. But if the horse was responding and I wasn't going to get to the wire until I did get into him a little more, then yeah, I'd be a little more aggressive and hit him a few more times than I'd hit the average horse.

Every once in a while I'd hit a horse in the wrong spot — they have an area underneath their hip where there's some soft skin — and I'd cut them up or leave a mark or a welt. I'd feel badly about it: I was very uncomfortable if I got off the horse and I saw it with a welt or a cut. When I rode in California — after leaving Canada to race full-time in the U.S. at the end of the Woodbine autumn meet in 1978 — McCarron and I once tied for the title of best rider with the whip. (In California, they rated jockeys as the best coming out of the starting gate, the best with the whip, the best rider covering a certain distance and the best rider on the dirt.)

As far as the suspensions went, I wasn't the only one being singled out on the Toronto circuit. *The Globe and Mail* racing reporter Larry Millson noted that inquiries were becoming "a common thing" at Woodbine during this time period. Meanwhile, my threatened departure elicited an interesting column by the *Toronto Telegram*'s Bob Pennington:

My first thoughts were of sorrow because he is an admirable young man in so many respects. Unscarred, it had seemed, by success, always courteous, with a quiet charm that typified a much earlier generation, and yet showing fashionable independence by growing his hair long because he liked it long, whatever the snarling reaction of racing's old guard. The loss to Canadian racing would be of a remarkable horsemen, blessed with immense natural gifts, tremendous resolution and an unobtrusive courage indispensable to consistent victories at the track.

Why should there be one set of racing rules for a Sandy Hawley any more than hockey's judiciary should show special tolerance to a Bobby Orr? Or was the idol of Whitby merely trying to suggest that he had been singled out by the stewards for special attention? Whatever the motivation, Hawley's reported disenchantment with Ontario seemed remarkably unlike the all-Canadian boy who had always insisted on putting Canada first, however tempting the offers that flowed from the United States.

Eventually, I cooled down. After talking to Colin Wick, I decided to stay in Ontario for the balance of the season. However, the stewards' decisions did not go unnoticed. Larry Millson wrote that the Woodbine summer meet would be remembered for the jockeys' claims of foul and the stewards' inquiries: "The stewards have been reviewing more movie footage than an Ontario censor previewing a Russ Meyer film festival."

Ronnie Robinson:
He was given a lot of breaks. The way Sandy rode, any time he got [suspensions] he could have gotten them five, six, eight times before that. The stewards used to give him some breaks. If it was even close they gave him a break on it. The obvious ones, they had to nail him on.

He was riding, like, nine or ten horses a day and he was just a young kid learning. He never meant to do things wrong, but he'd just run into situations where he'd get a horse running and he'd drive through anywhere, or drop over on somebody and duck in to go on the inside of somebody else, or hit somebody to drive them out so he could get out around the horse.

Every jock in the jocks' room was looking for him. Any time you get a kid that's riding four or five winners a day, everybody's looking for him out there, especially all the old riders. He used to take his shots, and he got away with a few of them, but he'd get nailed and that was all there was to it. The stewards were more than fair a lot of times.

I also ran into trouble with the stewards at Monmouth Park in New Jersey when I rode Kennedy Road there in a race in late July. He had so much speed that he would come flying out of the starting gate and wouldn't change leads — or switch from leading with the right leg to the left, to make it easier to round a turn. If a horse doesn't change leads, it will sometimes drift on you. I couldn't get Kennedy Road to change leads, and going into the first turn at Monmouth Park he almost made a right-hand turn. I ended up taking out a couple of horses with me. I won the race but was disqualified and placed fourth for causing interference in the stretch. The stewards will often look at that, and if they believe the rider is at fault and could have done more to prevent the horse from doing what he did, he'll get suspended. But when Kennedy Road tried to get out that day, I was standing up on him trying to make him make the turn.

Less than two weeks later, I rode Kennedy Road in the Monmouth Invitational, but finished fifth. I also rode Lauries Dancer at Saratoga in the Alabama Stakes, a major race on the North American calendar for three-year-old fillies. The card attracted a crowd of 28,345, the second-largest in the racetrack's long and storied history. The bettors among that crowd overlooked Lauries Dancer, dismissing her at odds of almost 13–1. She broke furthest from the rail in the field of eleven and lost a lot of ground. I was in the middle of the pack on the backstretch, about seven lengths off the lead, but I began to advance steadily and overpower the opposition, ultimately winning by three lengths.

Kennedy Road also ran that weekend, placing second in a seven-furlong prep for the Travers Stakes at Saratoga in upstate New York. He was wearing blinkers to make him focus better for the first time and clocked six furlongs in a blistering 1:09, but he tired in the final sixteenth. The race was run in a track-record time of 1:21 2/5.

A week later, a record crowd of 30,011 came out for the Travers, in which Kennedy Road faced his biggest challenge yet: Bold Reason, who had run third in the Kentucky Derby and Belmont Stakes and was in the midst of a winning streak. Kennedy Road blistered the opening three-eighths of a mile in 34 seconds and led by eight lengths after half a mile, but the pressure of maintaining that pace proved too great; he eventually faded to fifth while Bold Reason registered his latest victory. Mr. Bentley told the media that the blinkers might have been a mistake, and the fact that it was the horse's fourth hard race in a month was also an issue. The blinkers did cause Kennedy Road to show a little too much speed. He was the type of horse that would get out there and go a little too quick in the first part, then kind of flatten out. But he was also a little too hard to control. When he got out there, if he could see another horse he'd try and come back on, but with the blinkers he couldn't see any other horses around him.

Fifteen days later, Kennedy Road ran on the grass in the Prince of Wales Stakes and, at less than even odds, came in third by a head and neck. He'd led by a length in the stretch, but weakened slightly in the final sixteenth to the wire. New

Pro Escar, who came into the race with one win in eleven starts but whose trainer felt he had improved significantly on the grass, won at almost 50–1 odds.

On the plus side, Lauries Dancer won her next race, the Delaware Oaks, her seventh victory in twelve starts that season.

On November 26, as the Canadian racing season neared its conclusion, I experienced an embarrassing moment on a day that began with such promise. I won four of the first seven races on the Greenwood card, but the eighth and final race is one I'll never forget. It had been an extremely long year, and on this occasion I didn't even look at the distance of the race, which was a mile and three-quarters. That's a long and rarely run distance, and in this case it required two full laps of the track. I was aboard Sylcon, the 3–2 second choice in the field of five, which included a two-horse entry that was the favourite at 3–4 odds. For some reason, I had it in my mind that the race was seven-eighths of a mile because I was coming out of the starting chute for a race that length.

As I came through the stretch, I was in front; if I hadn't been in front, I probably would have thought, "Why aren't these other jockeys riding harder than they are?" I made the lead at the head of the stretch, whacked my horse a couple of times and looked back. As I drew away from the field, I just kind of put the whip away. The crowd was going wild, and I was thinking, "Wow, a lot of people must have bet on this horse." I stood up at the wire and let my horse drift out a little bit, as jockeys do so that the horse will relax and we can get them to pull up. I still couldn't figure out why the crowd was so excited; I looked down on the inside and saw the other riders still crouched down on their horses. Instantly I realized what was happening. "Oh, my goodness," I thought to myself, "it's a mile and three-quarters and we have to go around again!"

I let my horse get back into the race, of course, and I finished last by sixteen and a half lengths. It was very embarrassing and I felt badly for the owner and the trainer. Fortunately, they were good about it. I would go on to win with that horse the next year. Still, the fans got on me pretty good. The ones who hadn't bet on the horse weren't too bad, but the ones who had were, understandably not at all happy. I could see their point, one hundred percent. It was probably one of my most embarrassing moments as a jockey.

Although I'd got off to a sluggish start, I concluded the Canadian racing season with 338 winners in Ontario and 349 overall. I placed second in North America in wins to Laffit Pincay Jr., who had 380. Laffit led the earnings parade with more than $3.7 million, while my mounts, at $1,195,515, placed seventeenth overall.

The year 1971 took me from one extreme to the other, from the low point of the troubles with Tom Hays to the highlights of seeing Lauries Dancer win Canadian horse-of-the-year honours and Kennedy Road take the crown as the nation's top three-year-old. It was very emotional, very stressful, but it ended up being a super year, and I have Art Stollery to thank for that.

CHAPTER FOUR

Going for the Record

I don't recall exactly when I met my first wife, Sherrie Tuckie. She grew up in Hamilton, the daughter of a couple who were both animal-rights activists. She had a passion for horses; she began riding at age eight and had her first show jumper four years later. She quit school in 1964, at sixteen, to work at the track full time. She exercised horses in the morning for trainer Ted Mann and supplemented her income in various other ways, including ponying racehorses in the post parade. I was too shy to ask for her phone number, so I had my valet, Ronnie Robinson, ask on my behalf. He told me she was a bit older than I was, but that didn't matter to me because I was attracted to her.

> *Ronnie Robinson:*
> He was still pretty shy, and when he saw a girl he liked he'd come to me and he'd say, "Boy, I'd really like to take her out," so I'd approach the girl and say, "Hey, you want to go out with The Kid?" I was galloping horses freelance at the time, and I was getting on so many that I'd get Sherrie, who was also freelance galloping, to handle my overload every morning. I'd known Sherrie for a long time. When Sandy told me he wanted to go out with her, I told him she was a nice enough person.

I started off the '72 season in Florida, then returned to Ontario in the third week of April for the Fort Erie meet, which had already begun. Once again I had long — shoulder-length — hair and a thick moustache. And that became as much a topic for conversation as my riding. As *Toronto Sun* columnist Jim Coleman wrote:

His hair, which hangs to his shoulders, would make one hell of a nice nest for an entire family of red-breasted robins. Some old-fashioned critics suggest that Hawley resembles Rip Van Winkle riding a park policeman's runaway horse. Nevertheless, as surely as the Good Lord created little mushmelons, Sandy gets the job done on the racetrack.

It's funny when I think about it now. Long hair was just in style then and I felt comfortable with it. I always figured that, as long as you keep it clean and take care of it, it shouldn't really have been a problem with anybody. And I really took good care of my hair, getting it trimmed often and washing it all the time. Colin Wick used to say it was really frustrating: everybody else would be out of the jocks' room and I'd be there for half an hour drying my hair. Colin also said I looked like General Custer — I took that as a compliment.

I won the Fort Erie meet despite my late start, and when the meet shifted to Woodbine, I posted some impressive personal marks. On the Victoria Day holiday weekend in May, I won the three feature stakes races: the Marine on Saturday, the Swynford on Sunday and the Ultimus on Monday. I won seven of the nine races that day, a personal best for victories on one card. One of the winners was Sylcon, the same horse on which I'd had that embarrassing moment at Greenwood the previous fall, when I misjudged the distance of the race.

I had a lot of days when it looked like I could win a lot of races. Sometimes you'll win one or two and think you were on some pretty live horses; if you win four, you'll think that's going to be it for the day; but when you win seven races on one card it's just unbelievable.

The newspapers were keeping daily tallies of my winners — 23 in 40 mounts and 42 in 82 races. Again, I wasn't caught up in all that stuff. "I don't care if the young son-of-a-buck lets his hair grow until it hangs right down to his heels," trainer Frank Merrill Jr. told Jim Coleman. "I'm willing to bet that Hawley could make a Model T Ford wake up and beat a Cadillac in a six-furlong sprint."

Coming from someone who would become a Hall of Famer, that was a fantastic compliment. Frank Merrill was such a classy guy and so wonderful to be around. Even when I'd be finished with morning workouts, I'd love just to go by his barn and hear him talk about racing — he was a fascinating guy to listen to.

Mr. Coleman also noted that my riding style had changed perceptibly from my early days.

> Today's Hawley is a rootin', scootin' hell-for-leather cavalryman who is all over his horse's back in the manner of an agitated centipede. But he's winning more races than any other jockey who ever came down the pike in Canadian racing — and winning is the name of the game in the horse business.

Now, that observation is interesting, because I don't feel like I really changed my style until after I went to California full time in 1978. Maybe when I first started riding I wasn't as active on a horse, but once I started getting more comfortable, I guess I did get more bouncy — kind of all over the horse — and more aggressive. At one point, the great Avelino Gomez said, "Sandy, I want to bring it to your attention, I think you're getting a little too bouncy on a horse — a little too aggressive." I paid attention to that tip and I settled down a bit. Even later on in my career, if it was going to be a close finish, I would just try and lay out flat on the horse. Gomez used to do his kidney bouncing in the last seventy yards down to the wire — that would really make a horse respond and, I think, stretch out to its fullest. In one race, I was coming down the stretch and I was bouncing so much that I bounced right off the back off the horse! Everybody asked me what had happened, and I blamed it partially on my valet, Ronnie Robinson — I said he'd got me a brand new pair of riding boots and we'd forgotten to scrape the bottoms. Sometimes when you get brand new boots, they're really slippery, so you scrape the bottom of the boots to give them some grip. But that's not why I slipped out of the stirrups that day: I was doing so much kidney bouncing that I bounced right off the back and landed on the ground. It was right at the wire, and the first thing I said was, "Did I win the race?"

Ronnie Robinson:
He was really practising that Gomez bounce at the time and he got to bouncing too much. When he went to come up, just coming to the wire, he went right over the side of the horse. Of course, everybody made a big fuss about it, and as he came back I laughed at him and said, "You bounced your way right off that horse." "No," he said, "it was those boots."

Gomez used to throw his butt back out and hit a horse on his kidney and hit him three or four times. He always caught him within the seventy-yard pole because a horse would take two or three strides to pick up again — and then he'd come up out of there and just fire for the next seven or eight strides. He'd just extend himself like you couldn't believe. Sandy had seen him do this — Gomez had beaten him a few times with that one — so Sandy was trying to learn it, and he did learn it, but never to the point that Gomey could do. He could go so far on a horse's kidneys, it was unbelievable. Sandy accomplished it, but it was when he was still trying to learn that he came off and tried to blame the boots.

He used to switch boots during the card. He'd ride two or three races, then I'd pull the boots off and put some fresh boots and pants on because he always tried to look his best going out. He didn't look like a rag-bag at any given time. It was all about presentation and looking good going out there — presenting himself to owners and trainers and looking good on a horse. I used to have a big blacksmith's rasp that I'd use to rough up the soles of the boot in the toe section because Sandy used to ride strictly with his toe in the iron.

In 1972, I won my third consecutive Canadian Oaks aboard a horse called Happy Victory. Veteran trainer Dave

Brown, whom I always loved riding for because he was such a great guy, called it the high point of his career. After that, I was hoping to win my third Plate. Early in the season it appeared that my best shot would be with Gentleman Conn, whom I had ridden regularly the year before. He was the champion two-year-old colt or gelding in Canada. I also had another prospect in George Gardiner's Henry Tudor, who had five wins in six races on the season. I had ridden Henry Tudor in his only meeting against Gentleman Conn in the Marine Stakes, and Henry Tudor won by half a length.

Gentleman Conn lost a race on the road to the Plate, but my sense was that he didn't get a hold of the track. There was a chance to bounce back in the Plate Trial. It had two divisions, and I rode Parkrangle to victory in the first division and finished second in the other with Gentleman Conn. I stayed inside for most of the trip, but found myself in tight quarters early in the stretch and bumped the rail twice before the final eighth of a mile. I then swung outside for running room, but bumped into Henry Tudor with about a sixteenth of a mile to go and finished three-quarters of a length back of Barachois. The stewards posted the inquiry sign, and after reviewing the replays of the race they disqualified Gentleman Conn and placed him fourth.

Gentleman Conn was a luggin'-in son of a gun. He was a huge, strong horse — so strong that I could hardly control him some times when he was lugging in. If he only would have run straight he would have been a better horse. When he came up down the stretch and moved towards other horses, he would lug in so badly that I couldn't even ride him. I was trying to hit him left-handed in the Plate Trial, but he lugged in so badly that I bothered Henry Tudor. I received a ten-day suspension for what the stewards deemed careless riding — they didn't think I'd made enough effort to keep him straight. But if Gentleman Conn had been the type of horse that ran straight, I wouldn't have had a problem.

Steward Eric Barber told the *Daily Racing Form*'s Wally Wood, "Hawley is the leading rider on the circuit, but if he commits an offence he must pay the penalty. It's just an unfortunate incident." Fellow steward John Damien added:

Sandy made a judgement call. He elected to go between Barachois and Henry Tudor and if he hadn't come in so quickly he might not have bumped Henry Tudor — but he did.

The suspension was set to begin June 17 — Queen's Plate day. I decided not to appeal the suspension, which denied me the chance to try to win an unprecedented three consecutive Queen's Plates to go with three consecutive Canadian Oaks victories. I might well have won an appeal, but I knew the stewards had a tough job to do. Talking to Colin Wick about it, I said, "I just want to have a clean slate of never appealing."

Ronnie Robinson:
I said to Sandy, "Maybe ten times you should have got a suspension and you got away with it. Take what you've got coming and go and enjoy the time off."

To take my place, trainer Jerry Meyer recruited an American-based jockey, John Baboolal, to ride Gentleman Conn. He had ridden the horse a couple times that season. The crowd of 34,367, the largest in Plate history, made Gentleman Conn the favourite in the field of fifteen at just under 3–2 odds. Owner Saul Wagman decided that I would collect 10 per cent of whatever Gentleman Conn won in the race — basically what I would have earned if I had ridden in the race. He didn't have to do that. I had ridden some races for him in the past, but he was wonderful to me when it came to that.

I sat in the owner's box of Saul Wagman and watched the race with Sherrie. It felt uncomfortable not to be on a horse, to be a spectator at a race of that magnitude. I was wishing I could have had the mount, but I was definitely cheering for John Baboolal. As it turned out, Victoria Song, who hadn't won in thirteen starts as a two-year-old and didn't win his first career race until almost two months before the Plate, chalked up the upset. Robin Platts, who also had Colin as his agent, was aboard for the win — his first of what would be four trips to the Plate winner's circle in his career. Gentleman Conn ran third by two and a half lengths, racing from far back and making a move on the outside in the stretch, but lacking a closing bid.

* * *

In July 1972, Sherrie and I married at Islington United Church. It was my first time, her second. We walked down the aisle together and exchanged vows that we had written ourselves. I wore a black velvet suit with a shirt that had a jabot of French lace that came down the front and frilly cuffs — kind of an Edwardian look. I thought it looked good with my long hair, and it was back in the days when people were being a little bit different and expressing themselves differently.

Sherrie Hawley:
Sandy really liked the rock bands in those days, and I think that was a bit of a style that maybe some of the rock bands wore. That was just kind of how he dressed in those days. I wore an ivory, lace dress with peach lining, and my bridesmaids had peach dresses.

My best man was Louis Hutchison, with whom I'd shared a tack room when I first came to the track in 1968, and with whom I'd later roomed in a hotel and then an apartment. We were best friends for many years. Sherrie and I had already moved into a four-bedroom, 2,700-square-foot house we had purchased prior to our wedding. Real estate agents showed us around various houses, but we didn't like any of them. Then we came across one in Mississauga, about a twenty-five-minute drive from Woodbine. It was one of only four on a street that was largely undeveloped. The house we bought was the model home, and it was grey, which Sherrie and I always liked. We paid $60,000 for it, but it really escalated in value when the real estate boom took off in the next decade. We hired a decorator — her name was Christine — to furnish the house with art objects yet also make it comfortable and relaxing. The décor was a long way from my old apartment, with my posters of Led Zeppelin and other bands and the black lights.

* * *

I went on to win the Woodbine meet with 83 victories from 279 mounts, then followed that up by taking the Fort Erie meet with 55 wins in 210 mounts. When the circuit shifted back to Woodbine, I prevailed again, winning 79 of the 263 races. I was in a battle for the North American championship with Laffit Pincay Jr., who had claimed the title the year before. I overtook him in early October and never surrendered that lead, taking the Greenwood meet with 67 wins in 201 mounts. I finished the Canadian season with 318 wins, and my U.S. victories brought that up to 347 overall.

Rather than go to Florida that winter, Colin and I decided I should try the Maryland circuit. It was one of many great decisions Colin made for me in my career. One of the trainers he connected me with was Dick Dutrow, who was looking for someone to ride on a first-call basis for him. I just happened to be in the right place at the right time. I won 11 races in the first two weeks, and 20 overall, for a year-end total of 367 wins, by far the most in North America. Pincay placed second with 78 fewer wins, but again his mounts were more lucrative, earning more than $3.2 million compared to my $1,361,342.

As 1972 gave way to 1973, Colin and I had a New Year's drink at our residence, the Ramada Inn. We'd had a great year and Colin said, "How about we try to break Bill Shoemaker's record of 485 wins in a season and try and get to 500?" Having had a drink, and not thinking about the work ahead of us, I said, "Yeah, let's give it a go. Let's try and win 500 races."

Colin told the media, and the writers all thought we were slightly nuts. On New Year's Day I won two races; at the end of the day Colin came up to me and said, "We only have 498 to go." I'd kind of forgotten the goal we'd set the night before. "What do you mean?" I asked him. "We're going for 500 winners, right?" was his reply. "Okay, Colin," I shrugged, "let's go for it."

Around the same time, I was the subject of a story in *Sports Illustrated* titled "Should He Stick to the Sticks?" One aspect of the article bothered me: "There are those who declare Hawley has yet to prove himself a top jock, never mind *the* top jock, because he does not compete regularly at New York or Florida tracks."

I felt I could go anywhere and ride with anyone if I got the mounts. But while Laurel, Maryland, wasn't New York or Florida, it was big racing in those days. I was happy to go there. Colin had made that decision, and I stuck with him on it. And it ended being the right decision, because business went very, very well for us in Maryland. Then we had a chance to go ride in Arkansas.

Colin Wick:
I got a phone call from Oaklawn Park in Hot Springs, Arkansas, from Doug Davis, the leading trainer there. "Why don't you come here and ride first call for me?" he said. I put it to Sandy: "Let me get back to Doug and see what kind of retainer we can get."

 We started thinking about it, and I said, "If you go there, he's the leading trainer, so you could be leading rider. Let's go and try and break 500." Sandy said, "If you want to do it, let's go. If it doesn't turn out, we can go home to Woodbine." But the bottom line was always thinking about coming home.

We rode four horses for Doug Davis on opening day and won with all of them. From there, our business just took off. Doug was a big, tall cowboy — even wore the hat — and at first he wouldn't even come down to give me instructions because of my long hair. Well, that changed when I started winning races, and trainers and owners came down to the paddock to ask about putting me on their horses.

Colin Wick:
Doug Davis said to me, "Can you get him to cut his hair?" I said, "Cutting his hair ain't going to make him ride any different."

 "I know," he said, "but I've got to face these cowboys. They keep asking me why I keep riding the long-haired jock — he looks like a girl."

 I said, "I'm not going to tell him to cut his hair. That's personal. If he wants long hair, if he wants a moustache, that's his business."

John Lively beat me for the Hot Springs riding title on the last day, but I'd left about three weeks before that to return home for the start of the Greenwood meet because we were all homesick. After spending so many months in motels and apartments, Sherrie and I settled into our new home. In addition to furniture and appliances, by now we had acquired a variety of pets, including a Dalmatian pup named Sheba, two stray cats named Buttons and Bows, and two lovebirds named Bobbie and Billy. We also had two horses boarding at a farm — an aging thoroughbred named Honey, whom Sherrie had ridden for show jumping before retiring her, and a younger thoroughbred we bought in Maryland to convert into Sherrie's next show jumper.

I changed my look slightly, shaving off the moustache but maintaining my long hair — not that it had any bearing on my riding. In a three-week period, we won 27 of 87 races and finished first in the meet with 38 winners from 117 mounts. After the Greenwood meet, the Ontario circuit switched to Fort Erie, where we won 36 of 156 races. On the opening day of the Woodbine meet, I bagged four winners, and twelve in the first week. As usual, I was gearing up for the Canadian classics, but it didn't appear that I had the favourite for the Canadian Oaks this time. La Prevoyante, who had dazzled the North American racing scene the year before, winning all twelve of her races en route to being named the Canadian horse of the year and the top two-year-old filly in North America, appeared to be the favourite to win the Oaks. Although she had lost two of her first four starts on the season, she rebounded with two easy victories. In her last race leading up to the Oaks, she beat a field that included colts and geldings in the Quebec Derby.

My mount, Square Angel, had only run three times that season and had a win and two seconds. I had been aboard for all those races, the longest of which was seven-eighths of a mile, and now she had to run an extra quarter mile. Frank Merrill Jr., who trained the filly for Preston Gilbride, had worked Square Angel a hard mile since her last race to give her some foundation. He had her just perfect for that race — she was peaking.

Of the field of nine, La Prevoyante appeared to have a distinct advantage in class and fitness, having run a mile and an eighth in her last start, and the bettors made her the 1–20 favourite — the lowest possible odds. She led by nine lengths after half a mile and expanded it to twelve lengths after three quarters of a mile, run in 1:09 2/5, only two-fifths of a second off the track record for that distance. To put this into put perspective, she was running with the same kind of speed as a Kennedy Road. But she started to tire under the hold of her regular jockey, John LeBlanc, who had to start riding her more aggressively. With about an eighth of a mile to the wire, Square Angel caught up to her after making an authoritative run. Square Angel won by a length and a half over Impressive Lady, followed by La Prevoyante, who suffered her worst defeat in nineteen career races.

Square Angel, who was sent off at odds of more than 6–1, posted one of the biggest upsets in Canadian horse racing history at that time. The winning time of 1:48 4/5 shattered — by one and four-fifths seconds — the Oaks record set two years before by my former mount, Lauries Dancer. It also came within a fifth of a second of the course record.

Down the backstretch, La Prevoyante looked to be running easily, but at the three-eighths pole, when I asked my filly to run, she started flying. To beat La Prevoyante was an enormous feat, and Frank Merrill deserved full credit. He had won the Canadian training title in 1971 — for the thirteenth time — and led the continent three times, but he called that win the highlight of his distinguished career.

Square Angel had not been kept eligible for the Plate, leaving me without a contending mount. I wound up with Victorian Prince, who had finished second to La Prevoyante in the Quebec Derby. The Plate attracted a record crowd of 40,137, some of whom had been attracted specifically by the presence of Queen Elizabeth II and Prince Philip.

Notwithstanding her loss in the Canadian Oaks, La Prevoyante still commanded favourite status at 7–5 come post time. There was no shortage of owners seeking to beat the fabulous filly; a field of seventeen contested the race. Owner Jack Stafford entered two horses: Royal Chocolate, who had won a division of the Plate Trial, and Good Port. Victorian Prince went postward at slightly more than 4–1 and didn't factor in the Plate, placing fourteenth by fourteen and a half lengths. Royal Chocolate won by five and a half on the slow and tiring track at staggering odds of more than 23–1, posting the biggest payoff in the Plate in thirty-one years. La Prevoyante finished eighth by ten lengths in the most disappointing finish of her career.

Despite the Plate disappointment, I had great success overall in the meet, posting 86 victories from 313 mounts. As July gave way to August, we were in hot pursuit of New Jersey–based rider Vince Bracciale Jr., who led the continent with 259 wins, about ten ahead of me. As the Fort Erie summer meet came to a close in early September, I won the Prince of Wales Stakes — the second leg of the Canadian Triple Crown — aboard Tara Road, who was one-third of a Jack Stafford–owned and Gil Rowntree–trained entry that finished one-two-three. I won three of the four stakes races on the holiday weekend that ended the meet; more importantly, I surpassed Vince Bracciale for most wins in the continent.

A few days later, we announced plans to ride seven days a week in hopes of achieving our goals of breaking Bill Shoemaker's record and posting 500 wins in a season. Colin realized we weren't quite on pace to hit 500, so he came up with the idea of me going to Maryland to ride at Bowie Racetrack on Mondays and Tuesdays, which were non-racing days in Ontario. Vince Bracciale would also be racing there. We rented an airplane and hired a pilot to fly me back and forth for the two-month period.

Colin recommended Maryland-based Bob Maxwell to book the mounts for me at Bowie; Colin could have done the job, but he would have needed to get working papers. It also made sense to hire a Maryland-based agent, since we'd set a horribly tough schedule for ourselves, going back and forth.

Sherrie Hawley:
It was very hard on Sandy — really tiring. Sandy was riding nine horses a day lots of times. I think Colin was a big help in keeping Sandy pressing on with it. Colin

once told me he said, "Sandy, after this is over and you get the record, they're never going to remember the name Colin Wick, but they're going to remember Sandy Hawley."

It was kind of a whirlwind time in my life and his life, too. In those days he had youth on his side. He was doing something he loved. He was a hero. It was tough, but he pushed on through.

One day I was blanked on the two cards and felt I'd gone all that way for nothing; but on the next trip I won four one day and four the next. I realized the value of what we were doing, and appreciated that Colin knew what he was doing.

Bowie's publicity department added to the hype and stoked the rivalry by handing out buttons that proclaimed "I'm for Hawley" and "I'm for Bracciale." As my lead widened, there came to be a run on the Hawley buttons. Also as I started to pull away, Vince decided to try and narrow the gap by riding in West Virginia at night. Vince was a tremendous competitor; simply a very good rider. Even though the competition between us was fierce, Vince and I liked each other. We weren't buddy-buddy to the point where we'd go out to dinner every night, but in the jocks' room we'd talk and joke around. He was a wonderful guy and a very nice, clean rider. He was reminiscent of Robin Platts at Woodbine.

Avelino Gomez figured I had a good shot at winning 500. He told reporters: "If he does what he's doing now, riding someplace else when there's no racing here [in Ontario], he's a cinch. Two a day, I figure, and he can't miss. Even if he winds up even after Greenwood ends, he's gonna go to Maryland and ride against this guy and all he's gonna see is Sandy's backside."

On October 18 at Woodbine, we reached the 400-win mark, which made me the first rider to accomplish that in two different years. I reached the milestone in the second race on the card, aboard a five-year-old mare, Mary Pat, in a $4,500 claiming race. She went postward as the 3–4 favourite and absolutely crushed the field, winning the mile race by five and a half lengths. By the time the card had ended, we had won five races.

Ten days later, the eyes of the international horse-racing world were on Toronto, where the brilliant Secretariat was to cap off his career in the Canadian International Championship Stakes at Woodbine. Secretariat's owner, Penny Tweedy, had chosen Canada in part because it happened to be the native country of both the horse's trainer, Lucien Laurin, and his rider, Ron Turcotte. The choice of the International was somewhat unusual in that it would be only the second grass race for Secretariat.

During his remarkable season, Secretariat had swept the U.S. Triple Crown, winning the final leg at Belmont Park in stakes- and course-record time, and by a whopping thirty-one lengths. However, he went on to lose two of his next five starts, alternating between winning a start and losing the next, which caused Mrs. Tweedy some concern. Then he won the Man o' War Stakes at Belmont, looking very strong and tying a course record. She wanted him to finish on a winning note, and did not want to have to run the colt again if he lost his next race.

The Canadian International looked like a good opportunity for Secretariat to go out a winner, and after inspecting the turf course the week before the race with Laurin, Mrs. Tweedy gave her official seal of approval for the colt to come north and race outside of the United States for the first and only time in his career. It was a coup for Canadian racing, for the Ontario Jockey Club, and for E.P. Taylor, who had built Woodbine into one of the finest international tracks in the world.

A few days before the International, Ron Turcotte placed first in a race at Aqueduct but was disqualified for causing interference. The next day, the stewards handed him a five-day suspension to begin in two days' time, which prevented him from riding in Secretariat's final race. Turcotte chose not to appeal the suspension because, like me, he made a policy of not challenging the stewards' authority. The decision as to who would replace Ron rested with Lucien Laurin. Colin put in a call on my behalf, but Laurin had already given the mount to Eddie Maple, who rode second-call for him behind Turcotte. The story goes that Mrs. Tweedy would have allowed me to ride the horse if Laurin hadn't given the call to Maple, and that we missed out by half an hour.

Because of the lure of Secretariat, the Ontario Jockey Club boosted the purse in the International from $75,000 to $125,000. I watched Secretariat come off the van at Woodbine and was awestruck by just how great he looked. Ron Turcotte came up to work him on the Marshall Turf Course, and I was out there with my camera filming this great horse. He was the best-looking, and flat-out best, racehorse I had ever seen to that point. He was so proud when he went out on the racetrack; I think he knew he was good.

The race attracted eleven starters, including Kennedy Road, whom I had ridden to victory in the 1971 Queen's Plate. He had been shipped to California after debuting with a win in Florida in the early part of the season. He posted three wins and two seconds in California before he was sent to Belmont Park to face Secretariat in an invitational stakes race. Secretariat won that invitational by three and a half lengths, while Kennedy Road placed sixth in the field of seven by fifteen lengths. Art and Helen Stollery then brought him back home to Woodbine, and he registered a track record for three-quarters of a mile in a race one week before the International. Avelino Gomez had been aboard him for that win and retained the mount for the International.

We had the mount on E.P. Taylor's Presidial, whom I had ridden his last three times out. Presidial had also raced largely in California, and I first rode him in a stakes race in April. It was my first time in California, and I had little luck with Presidial, finishing fifth in the seven-horse race. Presidial was sidelined after that and did not race again for several months. He ran twice at Woodbine, finishing second the first time and third the next, both as the heavy favourite with me in the irons.

Weather-wise, the day of the race was miserable. It was overcast, misty and foggy. It was also cool — you could see the steam coming out of the horses' nostrils when they ran. In the jockeys' room we were joking that it was so dark that we should don miners' caps to ride in the International. But the chance to see the great Secretariat attracted a crowd of 35,117.

I had eight mounts on the nine-race card, winning two of the first three. I scored a third victory in the race before the International, cruising to a six-length lead aboard Conn

Smythe's Lovely Sunrise. As soon as the results of that race had been removed from the infield tote board, the money began to pour in on Secretariat. The bettors pounded him down to 1–5, many of them wagering simply to have a souvenir ticket regardless of the outcome. Kennedy Road commanded second choice at slightly more than 9–1, while Presidial went postward at more than 23–1. By the time of the race, darkness had descended. Kennedy Road forged to the front and bumped Secretariat twice down the backstretch. Kennedy Road led through the opening mile in a comfortable 1:37 3/5. Secretariat stalked him closely the entire way before Eddie Maple called on him in the backstretch and began a duel with Kennedy Road on the far turn. Secretariat took command thereafter, leading by twelve at the top of the stretch. With only the lights of the infield tote board to offer any illumination, Secretariat came home with a comfortable six-and-a-half-length lead. He ran the mile-and-five-eighths race in 2:41 4/5, only four-fifths off the course and stakes record set by The Axe II ten years before. Presidial was a nice horse, too, but the closest we could get was fourth. Kennedy Road faded to ninth.

The meet shifted to Greenwood, where, on November 19, I eclipsed my previous best of 452 single-season wins. Observers began speculating that I might set the world record at Greenwood if I could average three wins in each of the remaining eleven cards. I knew it would be tough to do, and though I wanted to set the record at home if possible, I couldn't keep up the pace. On November 30, the second-last day of the Ontario racing season, I failed to win a race, leaving me at 473. Ontario Jockey Club publicist Bruce Walker told the *Toronto Sun's* sports editor, George Gross, that I usually responded with a multiple-win day immediately after I'd been blanked, and he figured I'd win three or four on the last day at Greenwood. He was almost right: I won five. Among the wins, I booted home Fabe Count to a fourteen-length triumph in the Valedictory Stakes. I told the media afterwards that he ran "almost like Secretariat."

Sherrie Hawley:
He was such a competitor. If he ever went into a bit of a slump, which everybody does, he used to say to me, "I'm not going to change anything. I'm just going to keep doing what got me there in the first place," and eventually it always would work out. But he used to hate to get beat.

Two days later, at Laurel in Maryland, we resumed the pursuit of Shoemaker's record, now only seven wins away. I won with three of six mounts on my first day, and recorded three more the next day, to trail the record by a solitary win. The Ontario Jockey Club flew in some of my family and friends on the organization's private plane, but by the time everyone had passed through customs, the racing had already concluded for the day. My father arrived later on a commercial flight; he had just started a new job and hadn't intended to fly down until later in the week, but I urged him to push his plans forward.

Fortunately for everyone — and this included a horde of Canadian media — I didn't break the record that day, coming up short with eight mounts. Some of the newspaper stories in the next day's papers noted the irony of the name of the last horse I rode, I Will Do It, given the fact that I didn't.

The record finally fell on December 6, 1973, in front of family, friends and a crowd of 8,549 — but not without incident. I tied the record with a $4,000 claimer called Bold King, who won by three-quarters of a length in the third race of the card. In the next race, I was scheduled to ride Red's Landing, trained by Dick Dutrow, and as we were coming into the post parade, I tied the reins in a knot because they hung down a little too far. I hadn't even put my feet in the stirrups, and as the pony boy reached over to grab her, she ducked away. He grabbed on the bridle and snatched her to bring her back, and somehow the bridle broke and the bit fell right out of her mouth. I didn't even realize what was happening; then she just took off, because she was afraid of the pony, and starting running the wrong way around the racetrack. My feet were out of the stirrups and I was trying to grab hold of her when I realized the bit had dropped down and was hitting her in the chest.

I wanted to hold up the reins because I didn't want everything to fall down and have her trip on them. By this time she was just flying down the racetrack, going so fast that I thought to myself, "I can't jump off, because if I do I'm definitely going to get hurt." When you're in spills and you fall off, it happens so fast that you can't think about it and you can't tense up; my thinking now was that if I jumped off I would be all tensed up because I could see it coming. So I just tried to bide my time. I talked to her, patting her on the neck to relax and slow down, and finally she started to slow down just a little bit.

I thought to myself that I wasn't going to be able to get her to stop, because a thoroughbred won't do that, but I decided that, when it reached the point where she had started to slow down enough that it might be safe to jump off, I would — a small detail, given that I'd never jumped off a thoroughbred before, of course. The bit was still flying back and forth; it hit her in the knee and she sped off again. "I'm dead," I thought again, because I stood no chance of jumping off now. She was heading towards one end of the track where a bunch of tractors used to grade the racetrack were stored. A sobering thought occurred to me. We'd worked so hard all year to get to this point, having just tied Shoemaker's — my idol's — record, and everything could be for naught if I were to get hurt on this horse. "I could be out for the rest of the season if I break something," I realized.

As Red's Landing headed towards the tractors, I vowed to myself that I wouldn't be there with her — I *would* jump off. Fortunately, she saw the turn and had enough sense to go around it. I was a bit relieved by that. Then, about three-quarters of the way around the turn, she started heading towards the outside fence, to the gap area where horses come on and off the racetrack in the mornings. I figured she was running back to the barns, which wouldn't be unusual, since horses are creatures of habit. As she headed towards the fence, which was now blocked off, I estimated that she would have to slow down a little bit to try and jump that fence.

And that's exactly what happened. She started slowing down as she approached the fence, and that was when I jumped off. I didn't want any part of going through the fence with her because I might get hurt even more. She ended up jumping the fence and knocking it down, but she didn't fall. She ran back to her barn and ended up unhurt. In fact, about a week or so later, I rode her in a race and she won.

I twisted my ankle a little when I jumped off; at the time, I thought I'd hurt it badly because I found myself limping slightly, but my leg actually ended up being fine. But it was a very scary experience. I didn't think I was going to die, but at the same time I was hoping against hope that I didn't get hurt and miss the chance to break Shoemaker's record. I was later told that, when Colin heard I was on a loose horse running the wrong way around the racetrack, he was running through the grandstand. I also heard he had a double Scotch after he found out I was okay.

I returned in the next race to ride aboard Night Train Lane, who was trained by Mort Hardy, who conditioned horses back home for the Toronto realtor Dave Mann. The horse was a hard-knocking $10,000 claimer, and I knew him, having ridden him in late October at Greenwood. Night Train Lane went postward as the 7–5 favourite. He was such a nice horse; I remember getting to the head of the stretch and thinking, "I've got it." It's a feeling you get when you ask a horse to run and he really accelerates. You feel like there's no way anybody can run fast enough to catch you. I peeked over my shoulder a little to see if anyone was coming and nobody was — that's a wonderful feeling. I probably rode Night Train Lane a little harder than I needed to, but at the same time it's important to make sure you're going to win. And he did, by six lengths. Sherrie and I were both good friends with Mort, who was a wonderful trainer and treated us very well, so it was good to win the record-breaker on one of his horses.

"Maybe it's fate that Sandy didn't get to ride Red's Landing," Sherrie told the media. "The Lord wanted him to break the record on a Canadian horse."

When I returned to the jockeys' room, I literally received a cold reception from the other riders: they showered me with four buckets of icy water, including one filled with soap. That's not uncommon; it's like when you win your first career race and the jockeys celebrate by showering you with ice-cold water or painting your private parts with black dye — that crazy tradition called blackballing — or, sometimes, both. It was a great jockeys' room at Laurel; they were a great bunch of guys.

That night, in the motel room Sherrie and I shared with our pets, we celebrated the record-breaking achievement with family and friends, including our parents, my Uncle Bill and Aunt Mary, Colin and his wife, Margaret, Bruce Walker, and some members of the media. We had purchased about ten bottles of champagne, which we'd put on ice in the bathtub earlier in the day in anticipation of the record falling. Of course, I couldn't drink too much; I had to ride the next day.

A *Toronto Sun* reporter, Connie Nicholson, interviewed Duke Campbell at his farm in Gormley, Ontario, about my achievement. "I didn't think he'd get this far," he said. "Pretty good, isn't it?"

Toronto Sun columnist Jim Coleman wrote that the time had come for me to take my tack to the U.S. on a full-time basis.

> As a devotee of Canadian horse racing, I will hate to see him leave our country, but the indisputable fact remains that in order to gain international fame in his profession, a jockey must go to the Big Apple. He must ride a winner of the Kentucky Derby or the Belmont Stakes. Ultimately he must be prepared to go to France to ride in the Prix de l'Arc de Triomphe at Longchamps or he must go to England to ride in the Ascot Gold Cup.

I was still aiming for 500 wins. I needed only thirteen more, and I had twenty-two days to win them in. I notched one of those wins four days later at Suffolk Downs in Boston in the North American Riding Championship. This was a three-race series against a group of riders that included Ron Turcotte, Braulio Baeza, Vince Bracciale Jr., and four riders from New England. Bill Shoemaker and Laffit Pincay Jr. declined

invitations because the promoters had tried to sign the riders
to contracts that would have prevented them from
participating in similar events backed by anyone else. Angel
Cordero Jr. and Jorge Velasquez agreed to participate, but
arrived too late from New York because of poor weather. It
rained quite a bit just before the races, leaving the track a
soupy, sloppy mess. First prize in the three-race, winner-take-
all series was $10,000 and Sherrie asked me, "If you win it, can
I get a new show horse?" I didn't think I had much of a shot
because there were so many good riders involved, but I
finished with a win, a second and a third and won it all.

I won at least one race a day leading up to number 500,
and received letters of congratulation from an assortment of
well-wishers, including a nun. On December 15, 1973, in
front a crowd of more than 12,000 at Laurel, I reached the
mark — and realized the goal we had set on New Year's Eve —
aboard a black seven-year-old gelding named Charlie Jr.,
trained by Dick Dutrow. He ran very gamely from just off the
pace and romped to a five-and-a-half-length score. The local
media dubbed me Sir Lancelot, which I took as a great
compliment.

Winning number 500 was the biggest thrill of my racing
career to that point — and it would remain so throughout my
thirty years in the saddle. The biggest thrill of my life came
with the birth of my first child, Bradley, and when I first held
him. I never thought that I'd have an opportunity in later years
to become a father, so that became the biggest thrill of my life
— running neck and neck with the birth of our second child,
Russell. But where my riding career is concerned, winning
number 500 is still the biggest.

The media inquired about my immediate future, in
particular where I planned to ride in the new year. "It's possible
I'll do all my riding next year in the United States," I said. "We
haven't decided. If I decide to ride in California, my home will
still be in Canada. I like the cities in the United States, but
home is home."

Less than a week after reaching 500, the first of several
awards started coming my way. I became the first jockey to win
the Lou Marsh Award, presented annually to Canada's top

amateur or professional athlete and voted on by newspaper editors and broadcasters. I beat out a stellar group, including the previous year's winner, hockey star Phil Esposito, and fellow jockey Ron Turcotte.

I was also honoured the following August, during the halftime of a Canadian Football League game between the Toronto Argonauts and Hamilton Tiger-Cats at CNE Stadium. I arrived in the stadium in a landau paraded by a mounted honour guard.

We finished 1973 with 515 wins, 112 ahead of Vince Bracciale Jr. Laffit Pincay Jr., whom I would engage in a spirited battle during the Hollywood Park meet in California in 1976, won his fourth consecutive purse-earnings title with $4,093,492, bettering the world record of $3,784,377 set two years before. Laffit also won the Eclipse Award as the top jockey, as determined in a vote by the *Daily Racing Form*, the Thoroughbred Racing Association and the National Turf Writers' Association.

I was a little disappointed about that, because after breaking Bill Shoemaker's twenty-year-old record and becoming the first jockey to win 500 races in a season, I thought for sure we would have won the Eclipse. I did, however, receive a Special Eclipse Award of Merit.

CHAPTER FIVE

California Calling

At the end of 1973, having won an unprecedented 515 races, I told Colin that I had to take a break because my body was telling me I had to stop. I was extremely tired and actually had a couple of sores on my head where I wore my helmet. In short, my body was breaking down on me and telling me I needed a rest. Colin replied that the trainers who had taken riders off mounts to put me on their horses were expecting me to ride until at least the end of the meet, early in the year. I just felt I couldn't continue, and we kind of got into a bit of an argument. I was in tears and so was Colin, who was like a second father to me, because he was torn. On the one hand, he understood I felt I needed to stop riding, but at the same time he knew we had a commitment to the trainers to continue riding. We were both very emotional about the situation.

We talked it over and decided I would ride to the end of the meet, but I didn't make it — about two weeks into the new year I ended up with double pneumonia. I went to the doctor, and I probably should have gone to the hospital, but the doctor made house calls to my hotel room, giving me shots. I was off for three weeks.

I'd had fourteen wins before the illness, and after recuperating I picked up where I'd left off and finished the Bowie meet as the winningest rider. I chose to come back home to ride, but first I took some time off, participating in a fox hunt in Maryland, then going to Las Vegas to unwind with Colin. My game of choice became keno — and the reason why is kind of a funny story. I had ridden a filly at Greenwood called Keno Girl, and I couldn't believe it when I found out they had a game in Las Vegas called keno and that there was a girl who came by and took your bet. I had never been to Las Vegas before, and I thought this was quite a hunch. I ended up making $300 on keno. To take the story even further, the first horse I rode back when I returned from Vegas was Keno Girl and she won again. I couldn't believe that coincidence. It was uncannny.

And on the subject of betting, over the course of my entire career I probably placed a bet about twenty times and maybe cashed one or two tickets. I remember losing a lot more than I ever won. I hardly ever bet because I just felt I didn't want the added pressure. If I was working a horse and I had a strong feeling about it, I might bet; otherwise, I didn't. People would ask me all the time about who I thought would win, but my standard reply today is, "I rode for thirty years, and if I knew who was going to win I wouldn't have ridden that long!" Sometimes friends would ask, "Who do you like today?" and I'd tell them, "I think this one has a chance." And I'd have to say that, roughly 50 per cent of the time it happened that the ones I overlooked ended up winning while the ones I'd recommended got beat.

When I came back from Maryland, the Ontario Jockey Club and I jointly sponsored a minor hockey team we called Hawley's Horses. The idea was initiated by a firefighter named Gary Leeman, who was a huge racing fan and who dropped by the jockeys' room and pitched the idea of sponsoring a team. I thought it was a great idea and got together with the OJC. Gary's son, Gary Jr., was the captain of the team. He was a defenceman, and was always the best player on the team, but who would ever have ever guessed that he'd go on to become a star in the National Hockey League? The Toronto Maple Leafs drafted him as a defenceman, but he was converted to a forward and he scored fifty goals one year. The younger Gary also became a horse owner, partnering with his Leafs teammate Ed Olczyk.

Hawley's Horses did well, and I remember having some good times watching them play. The team would often come to the races and watch me ride; I remember them all cheering me on to victory. Hawley's Horses won a championship in a tournament at Maple Leaf Gardens, and I stood behind the bench, wearing a team jacket, which featured a horseshoe crest and the number 515, symbolizing my victories from the year before.

I returned to racing for the Fort Erie spring meet and quickly notched my 2,000th career win. Around this time, I also received my first U.S. Triple Crown mount when trainer Charlie Wahler hired me to ride All Game in the Preakness Stakes in Baltimore. All Game had won only two of his ten starts and had finished second in his last outing. The oddsmaker made him 12–1 in the morning line. The favourite was Derby winner Cannonade.

Toronto Sun columnist Jim Coleman said it best: "All Game isn't a world-beater, but he's considerably better than an empty stall."

All Game finished eleventh in the field of twelve, almost eighteen lengths behind winner Little Current, who prevailed by seven lengths.

A month later, I rode in the Canadian Oaks and won for the fifth consecutive time, this one aboard Trudie Tudor, a horse who really sticks out in my mind. John Morahan, an Irishman who was such a wonderful guy, trained her and did a great job. I was a little concerned because, while she had a lot of speed, there were questions about her ability to maintain it at a distance beyond seven-eighths of a mile. Morahan took her to his farm and, in the European tradition of training, galloped her up and down hills. He put a lot of foundation into her — really legged her up, as they say at the track — and had her ready. All the credit goes to him for having her ready to go that distance of a mile and an eighth when she looked like she couldn't go over seven-eighths. I was pleased and excited to win for John because Trudie Tudor was one of my favourite horses. I think she was second or third or fourth choice in the betting — I had won five Canadian Oaks in a row, but had never ridden the favourite.

I had my choice of several Plate prospects and settled on George Hendrie's Native Aid, a winner of one of the two divisions of the Plate Trial Stakes. But my roan colt finished second by one and a half lengths to Amber Herod, who was basically running in midpack with me but who overtook my horse with a quarter mile to go and maintained his lead in the sloppy going. His trainer, Gil Rowntree, had been quoted as saying he relished an off track because he thought it would be the great equalizer between his horse, mine, and the favourite, Windfields Farm's undefeated colt Police Car, who had won the second division of the Plate Trial.

But Native Aid became another of my favourite horses because he always tried so hard. Almost two months later, I was aboard him in Fort Erie and guided him to victory in the Achievement Stakes, with Amber Herod running third. I had a banner day, winning with six of my seven mounts on the nine-race card. I came within a whisker of winning the seventh, finishing second by a length.

I enjoyed another personal highlight at Woodbine in October, when I posted six consecutive victories and seven overall on a card. It happened in the presence of the legendary rider Eddie Arcaro, who happened to be at the track to participate in a post-position draw for a stakes race. When the reporters asked Arcaro about my feat, he said, "It would be easier if I was asked what he does wrong, because he does lots of things good. I think he's a good rider and I really couldn't say if he does do anything really wrong."

Late that year, I represented Canada at an international competition in South Africa, coming up winless, but it was a fun trip. Because of the six-hour time difference, the first couple of days were tough, and the weather was very hot. Willie Carson, who was one of the top riders in England, proved to be a very funny guy, and we quickly struck up a friendship. He was always playing practical jokes. He and Ron Turcotte once pulled a prank on Colin Wick, who had joined me for the trip. Colin was a partyer and he loved to go out with the guys, whereas I was a bit of homebody. I'd have a couple of drinks and then get ready to go to bed, while others used to stay up all night, drinking and having a good time. So, one night Willie and Ron filled out an order form for breakfast and left it on the door of his room. Early the next morning, room service knocked on his door with breakfast. Well, he hadn't gone to bed until about 1:30 a.m. His wife, Margaret, answered the door, and in came a gentleman wheeling a trolley with a huge tray that included eggs Benedict, juice — and I think a couple of beers. Margaret said, "Colin, did you order all this?"

He said, "Hell, no, I didn't order that." When I heard about it later on, I asked Margaret what she did. "It was there and I was up so I ate it," she replied. She was a character, too, a wonderful woman.

I finished the season third overall in wins, with 373 from 1,283 mounts, but that paled in comparison to the output of a young apprentice phenom in Maryland named Chris McCarron, who in later years in California became one of my closest friends in the business. He shattered my year-old world record of 515 victories with 546. Bruce Walker, the publicity director at the Ontario Jockey Club, had been keeping me apprised of what was happening, and I was at Greenwood the day Chris broke my record. Shoemaker's record had lasted for so long, and I thought mine would last for a number of years as well. It was a shock, and a bit disappointing, to have it broken one year later. But then I recalled a conversation I'd had with Bill Shoemaker. "Mr. Shoemaker," I'd said, "I'm sorry I broke your record." "Jock," he replied, "records are made to be broken." Remembering that conversation, I took the same attitude. And of course Chris had *his* record broken in later years by Kent Desormeaux.

In 1975, we decided to take a chance and test the California circuit in the winter. Earlier in the year, while we were riding in Arkansas, Colin was approached by two representatives from the California racing circuit, racing secretary Lou Eilken and Bob Benoit, Hollywood Park's director of publicity. They showed Colin the condition book for Santa Anita and Hollywood Park and suggested that it might be a good idea if I tried the west coast. They were also trying to recruit Darrel McHargue, who was an apprentice at the time and who developed into an amazing rider. Benoit had first contacted us late in 1973, in between my breaking Shoemaker's record of 485 wins in a single season and my pursuit of 500. He had flown in from California to Suffolk Downs in Massachusetts, where I was riding in a jockey challenge. We later reconnected when I was invited to an all-star jockey challenge at Hollywood Park, and the dialogue continued with help from OJC publicity director Bruce Walker.

Bob Benoit:
Hollywood Park had been notably shy of riding talent behind Shoemaker (and later Pincay) because they were gone much of the year with the Triple Crown races. I had five riders I was after, and Sandy was at the top of the list. McCarron was on there, and so were Eddie Delahoussaye, Darrel McHargue and Jeff Fell. I eventually got four of them to move their tack to California. I got a very nice letter from Jeff saying how much he wanted to come and how much he appreciated my efforts, but he was going to take his agent's advice and stay in Florida. We got four out of the five, and three of them — Hawley, McCarron and Delahoussaye — are in the Hall of Fame, so it worked out pretty well.

The idea of going to the States full time had been in the back of our minds, but the thought of going to California and riding against the likes of Laffit Pincay, Bill Shoemaker, Don Pierce, Howard Grant and Jerry Lambert — holy cow! Never in a million years did we think we could go there and do well. LouEilken and Bob Benoit said that there were trainers interested in having us come, so that sparked our attention. We didn't know one person when we went there. We met a gentleman from Canada, Tiny Arnold, who I believed worked in the mutuels department, and he took us around and introduced us to all the trainers. There I was, trying to remember all these trainers' names — it got to be a bit mind-boggling. Bobby Frankel had been one of the top trainers in California, leading the Hollywood Park meet every year since his arrival from New York in 1972. His horses looked so good as I watched them do their daily work that I thought, "Wow, would it ever be great to be riding for this guy!"

Colin and I were taken to the press box, where we were introduced to the beat writers. I met several, but made an immediate impression on Gordon Jones, who worked as the writer and handicapper for the now-defunct Los Angeles *Herald-Examiner*.

Gordon Jones:
All of a sudden this good-looking, clean-cut choirboy, looking just beyond fit as a fiddle, plunked down beside me. And there was this old gentleman, his mentor, Colin Wick, with him. Colin sort of introduced me and Sandy was shy, but a complete gentleman. I talked with him and I thought to myself, "If I have ever seen the look of the eagles in any young man's eyes, this guy has it. I don't know what that is, but he's got it." Immediately I recognized, "Wow, this is somebody really different. He's got that reserve, that class, that gentlemanly stuff that's maybe more likely to come out of Canada than out of some of the hustling spots in America." You immediately liked the guy.

The very first day I walked into the jockeys' room it was like being among a bunch of movie stars. The California riders were as famous as any in the world, especially Bill Shoemaker, whose name I'd known since I was a little kid. I knew that Laffit Pincay was there, too. I'd raced against him the odd time before that, and I remember the first time I saw him in the jockeys' room. I was amazed at his upper-body strength. Howard Grant, Jerry Lambert, Wayne Harris — who was a Canadian — Don Pierce and others were in the room, but the person I was really looking forward to meeting and talking to was Bill Shoemaker. When I saw him, I walked over to him and said, "Mr. Shoemaker, it's nice to meet you. I've admired your career for years and I'm really looking forward to being here and riding with you." He said, "Sandy, just call me Shoe. It's good to have you here, and lots of luck."

What I didn't realize was that he was the biggest prankster in the whole jockeys' room. He used to like to dip a spoon in hot coffee and then sneak up and burn you on the neck. Guys used to get upset when he did that. I used to a little as well, but he was an idol of mine, so my reaction was practically "Oh, thank you, Mr. Shoemaker, for burning me on the neck." He also used to fill up your pockets with shaving cream; you'd get an unpleasant surprise after the races when you reached into your pockets.

The jocks' room at any track is full of pranksters — even the valets will keep you on your toes — but especially so in California. Shoemaker's greatest trick was to get an old banana and let it get really, really ripe, then peel it and put it in your pocket. You can imagine what that would feel like. One day a few years into my stay at Hollywood Park he went back to the jocks' room after finishing in the eighth race — everyone else was riding in the ninth — and turned on all the hot showers at full blast. By the time the rest of us got back there it was like a steam bath — you couldn't see to turn the taps off. Of course, the water was scalding hot, so it was painful to try to turn off the faucets. Everybody knew it was Shoemaker who did it; and even if he hadn't, we would have blamed it on him anyway. But we gave back as good as we got. Guys used to douse Shoemaker with buckets of cold water, fill his shoes with shaving cream or nail his shoes to the top shelf where the riders keep their boots. He'd go to pull them down to put them on, and they'd be nailed in place.

My valet was Jack Wood, who in his many years would work for some of the greatest riders — McCarron, Robbie Davis, McHargue, Steve Cauthen, Chris Antley. He worked for many of the Canadian riders when they shipped into California for a race — or, in my case, a whole bunch. And he still laughs at my long hair from those days. He still has some pictures of it.

The meet had already been underway twenty-one days when I became licensed to ride, and I was only getting on one or two mounts a day when I began. Our business started to pick up gradually — based in part on a sad and truly unfortunate incident. January 18, 1975, turned out to be one of the saddest days in the history of California racing. Alvaro Pineda, one of the all-time winningest riders on the California circuit and the leader at Hollywood Park in 1969, was killed in the starting gate before the fourth race at Santa Anita. His horse became fractious in the gate, and Alvaro's head was crushed against the steel bars, killing him instantly. He was only twenty-nine.

Colin and I went to the races that day, and I think we only had a mount in the last race, so we arrived a little bit late. There was mayhem by the jockeys' room. Lou Eilken came up

With Mom and
Dad, at age 7.

With Mom and
Dad, at age 16.

In 1969, my first full year of riding, with trainer Duke Campbell (*left*), and groom Doug Wilbur.

1971 Queen's Plate winner *Kennedy Road*, with trainer Jim Bentley.

At home with a number of my favorite trophies.

Pictured with contract-holder Tom Hays (*left*) and Hall-of-Fame trainer Frank Merrill (*right*).

Meeting Queen Elizabeth II, with E.P. Taylor in the walking ring at Woodbine, before the Queen's Plate.

Sharing a moment at Woodbine with long-time agent, Colin Wick.

Having fun with my idol Avelino Gomez.

In winner's circle on *Regal Embrace*, after winning the 1978 Queen's Plate, with owner E.P Taylor.

Michael Burns

Accepting first of two Lou Marsh Awards as Canada's Athlete of the Year in 1973.

Winning the 1978 Canadian International, on *Youth*, who may have been the best horse I ever rode.

Winning 1979 Canadian International on *Golden Act*, beating *Trillion*, ridden by another one of my idols Bill Shoemaker.

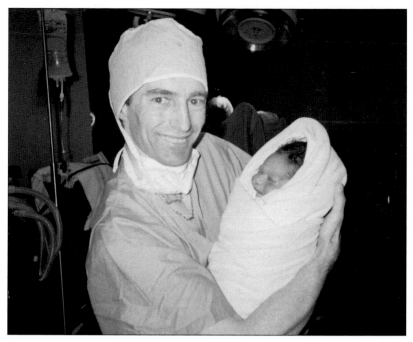

The birth of our first son, Bradley, May, 1992.

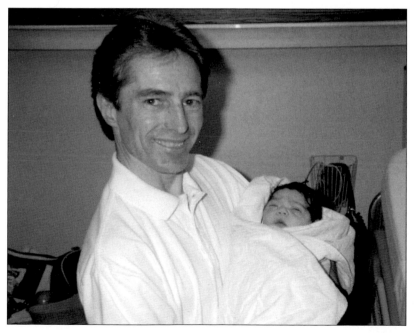

The arrival of our second son, Russell, April, 1994.

Celebrating in Saratoga with wife Lisa, and mom and dad, after being inducted into the *National Museum of Racing and Hall of Fame* in 1992.

With the plaque at the induction ceremony.

Coming to the wire in the milestone victory 6,000 on *Summer Commander.*

With family and friends, enjoying career victory 6,000.

At Bobby Orr's golf tournament, with friend Bobby Orr, and Stanley Cup.

Good friend Marty McSorley, and hockey fans Bradley and Russell Hawley.

Michael Burns

At the Community Association for Riding for the Disabled dinner, in my honor, with Colin Wick (*left*) and guest Dick Van Patten.

Fishing at Colin's cottage, with my father-in-law Isaac John.

Retirement Day
with Lisa, sons
Russell and Bradley,
and god-daughter
Ashley John.

Michael Burns

Making a speech
after my last ride,
with fellow riders.

Michael Burns

Cutting the cake after my last ride with David Gorman (Vice President of Corporate Affairs, Ontario Jockey Club) and Glenn Crouter (Director of Media Communications, O.J.C.).

Celebrating my retirement with Lisa, agent Colin Wick and trainer Duke Campbell (*right*) — the two gentlemen who contributed most to the success of my career.

On family vacation in Hawaii.

to us and said, "I think I have a mount for you in the stakes race." And we said, "What the heck are you talking about, the stakes race?" Well, Fred W. Hooper, who was one of the top owners, had a filly named Susan's Girl in the Santa Monica Handicap that day. Alvaro Pineda rode first call for him. I didn't know Alvaro well, because I'd just arrived in California, but a lot of the other riders were very good friends of his. It was very sad. A couple of the riders were so disheartened that they booked off the rest of their mounts — Laffit Pincay was one of them. Hooper mentioned to Eilken that he needed a rider, and Lou got me the mount. He said, "Sandy Hawley is a good, young rider. He just won 500 races." And Mr. Hooper said, "Well, put him on the horse."

Several jockeys and their wives were very upset about it, and there were some hurt feelings, but this was before they had gotten to know me. They saw me running into the jockeys' room to pick up the mount and thought, mistakenly, that I was all excited that a rider was hurt. But I wasn't enthusiastic — I was just hurrying into the jocks' room because I had to get into my silks, my boots and everything because there wasn't a lot of time before the race. Looking back, I can understand their reaction. It might have looked as though I wasn't showing proper respect for what had happened. In my defence, I wasn't fully aware of the whole situation yet. Fortunately, once the riders got to know me, they came to understand that I'd been misjudged.

I placed second by half a length, but I know Mr. Hooper was really happy with the way I rode her. Since he no longer had a first-call rider, I ended up riding a lot for him — and winning races. That caught the attention of some of the prominent trainers, including Bobby Frankel.

Bobby Frankel:
I wasn't happy with Pincay's agent [Vince DeGregory], so I got in touch with Colin Wick and asked him if Sandy wanted to ride first call for me. He was a leading rider wherever he'd been, so I took a chance on him. I didn't know too much about him, just that he won. He started riding for me, and he kept on winning.

Laffit Pincay Jr.:
My agent had a lot of problems with Bobby. They didn't
see eye to eye. We could be sitting at the same table
having dinner and they wouldn't speak to each other.
That's how bad it was. Bobby was winning all the races,
and I wanted to ride for him, but at the same time I
liked my agent. I was doing well with him and I wanted
them to get along, but they never did.

Sure enough, when Sandy showed up and started
winning races, he started riding some horses for Bobby
and winning. And since Bobby was having problems
with my agent, he just dropped me. It definitely helped
Sandy. When you ride for the best trainer — who is
winning all the races — it's a big advantage. Sandy
started winning all kinds of races and doing really well,
and everybody started talking about him.

Sherrie Hawley:
It happened almost overnight: people knew he was the
real deal. Nobody had really heard of him. Yeah, he'd
won 500 races, but nobody thought anything of that
because he did it in Canada and Maryland — big deal.
But when we went to California, all of a sudden we
were legit because we were winning races there. Now
everybody believed he was a great rider.

Gordon Jones:
When a new rider comes in, as handicappers and
racing fans, we watch their progress — or lack of same
— and we try to figure out if they're going to make it
and be the among the few that are good enough to stay.
We could see that Hawley was not getting the pick of
the litter — just like most newcomers — but son of a
gun, he was taking these longshots and bringing in way
more than his share.

Sherrie Hawley:
His style changed. When he rode in Ontario, he used
to bounce on the back of the horses. One time he said

he bounced right off. He told me that, if he bounced almost behind the saddle, the horse would kind of shoot forward, but when he was in California he stopped doing that. I think he probably just watched those guys. When Sandy came to California, it just seemed like it was magical.

Jack Wood:
He made an impression when he first came here because he could ride — and everybody wanted him to ride. He was a gentleman. You never heard him cuss or say a bad word or scream or holler. Everybody took to him. He was a likable guy and a good race rider. He'd hit a horse a lot when he got into a horse. He didn't always hit a horse that much, but if he got one that responded to the whip, he would hit him pretty good.

In California, when you start doing good, everybody wants you. I've seen riders come in here — like Angel Cordero Jr. when he was doing well back east, but when he came out here he didn't do any good. Nobody wanted to ride him. But when Sandy came here, everybody wanted to ride him — Mike Mitchell, Gary Jones, Bobby Frankel.

Gary Jones:
Bobby Frankel and I were stabled next to each other, and the first time we saw Sandy he came in with high-heeled boots and hair down to his shoulders — he looked kind of like a girl — and we laughed our butt off at him. We thought "This guy's never going to make it here," and by the end of the first week we were both trying to get first call on him. It was a tough circuit with small fields, so that's a big accomplishment.

He just was a great, underrated race rider. For as much as he got after a horse, he didn't kill one as much as people thought. He was more of a rat-tat-tat guy than blam, blam, blam. He'd just surprise a horse and they'd just freak for him. I saw horses do things with him that they couldn't do with anybody else, and I don't care who you put on them. If Sandy fit them, that was it. Nobody fit 'em better.

If you look at Sandy physically, he's not as strongly built as a Laffit Pincay. He's kind of an effeminate-looking guy, and when he hit a horse, he didn't kill one. It wasn't like that. He would just urge them. A lot of guys will hit a horse that many times and they'll stop running. Not with Sandy, because he wasn't hitting them that hard.

Gordon Jones:
He was probably the best man with the whip. I wouldn't say that he could transfer left to right and right to left quite as deftly as the others, but I sort of nicknamed him — and maybe somebody else beat me to it — the Gene Krupa of the jockeys. He could whip a horse in ways that nobody else even thought of. Not necessarily power, he could just use that whip so deftly, like Krupa with that fast drumming. Sandy Hawley was faster and quicker and more inventive. And he would do anything. He wouldn't welt the horse up and just beat them to death like some riders would. He probably didn't raise the welts as deeply as Pincay would with his famous power, but he'd do it in such strategic ways. He'd really get a lot of run out of the horse, and he could do it with his hands as well.

Everything was going well for us. Colin and I had got ourselves an apartment, and Bobby Frankel gave us pots and pans, bedding, dishes, silverware and so on. He claimed he was getting rid of it anyway because he'd bought a whole bunch of new household items. It was unbelievably generous of him.

Despite my late start, I placed in the top three in wins in the Santa Anita meet behind Bill Shoemaker and Laffit Pincay — and racked up stakes victories to boot. By this point there was a popular expression making the rounds among the horsemen: "Pincay Five Over or Hawley Five Wide." Laffit always battled his weight and routinely rode at 117 pounds, while I was making a reputation for winning by taking the overland route.

Laffit Pincay:
Horses that would not win for anybody would win for him. I had never seen a rider that could get more out of a horse than Sandy Hawley. His style was very different. He was quick with the whip. He wasn't really a strong rider, but he was very energetic. He was very active on a horse, and a lot of horses liked that. He didn't care about being wide — he would lose a lot of ground and still win races. I'm telling you I was really surprised at the way horses ran for him.

Gordon Jones:
As the meet went on, he continued to win with longshots. He'd be winning with the second-, third- or fourth-best horse, and pretty soon he was soon getting a few of the better horses. By the end of the meeting he was really going. We were saying, "He's finished Santa Anita. He's established himself. What's he going to do at Hollywood?"

Laffit Pincay:
I knew he was going to be tough there [at Hollywood]. He had a really good Santa Anita meeting. To me, Santa Anita is the toughest place to get mounts and to win races.

It was at Hollywood Park that things really clicked. Opening day attracted a record crowd of 37,601 and I won with five of seven mounts — including the feature, the Premiere Handicap, on High Rise, trained by Bobby Frankel for cosmetic king Sid Factor. I'll never forget that day. The next afternoon's Los Angeles *Herald-Examiner* jokingly referred to Hollywood Park as Hawley Park. It was a huge thrill, as big as when I first started riding in Canada and started to see my name in the top ten list in the program.

Gordon Jones:
I put that together — the Hawley Park reference — and I'm probably not the only writer who did. Our great sports editor, Bud Furillo, who was a genius at spotting angles, leaped on it.

I had a total of twelve wins in the first three days and it just kept going from there. Then, all of a sudden, immigration officials approached Colin and told him his working papers weren't in order — he wouldn't be able to work for me. I said, "He's my agent, and where he goes, I go. And if he's forced to go back to Canada, I'm going back to Canada as well." Marje Everett came to help us out, getting us a lawyer to represent us before the immigration officials. Though Colin didn't know anything about it, a number of people signed a petition on his behalf — including prominent horsemen, like trainers Charlie Whittingham and Ron McAnally. They argued that Colin had been my agent all along and hadn't taken away a job from anybody else.

Colin Wick:
There were three or four agents who said I was taking away a job. I wasn't taking their jockey away; I'd brought my own and he was a world champion. They got pissed off once I started doing well, and that's when they said, "Let's get this guy out of here."

The lawyer ended up getting Colin his working papers, for which all thanks belong to Marje Everett. John Mitchell took over as my interim agent, but I really wasn't going to stay in California without Colin. I would just as soon go back home and maybe return the next year. I just had that much confidence in Colin and the horses that he put me on. I wouldn't feel comfortable with anyone else but Colin booking mounts for me.

Sherrie Hawley:
Colin was unbelievable. When we were in California and the condition book would come out, there was a

room by the betting machines he'd go into and pick out all the horses he wanted to try to get on. And he knew every horse that was eligible for every race. He'd spend the next two or three days trying to get on those horses. Basically, his work was done after that.

He was amazing, just amazing. He used to say, "All I've got to do is find a horse that could be within five lengths of winning and Sandy will get it there." It was unreal how that guy just went into a strange place and got the mounts for Sandy — and, of course, once he had the horse, Sandy came through.

Sandy was one of the most natural riders I have ever seen. He got on the horse, and whichever way the horse ran, that's how he rode it. He was amazing that way. Nowadays, some of the trainers give the jockeys instructions on where to be at every pole, but that wasn't the way Sandy did it. He had a genius for conning horses on the lead. He could con them along and they just kept on going. It was amazing.

In those days, Sandy used to whistle at his horses to get them to run. Once, we were at a party given by Marje Everett, the vice chairman of the Hollywood Turf Club board and the majority stockholder of Hollywood Park, and I can always remember Laffit Pincay sitting there and he saying, "I couldn't believe it. I'd be in front and I'd hear that whistle and I knew he was coming." It was unbelievable — unstoppable, like a freight train.

I had great success around this time with a three-year-old colt called Native Guest, who had posted a four-race win streak. It prompted the horse's owner and trainer, Bobby Frankel, to point the colt to the Preakness Stakes, the second leg of the U.S. Triple Crown. This time it appeared that I had a better shot than the year before, when I rode All Game. I liked my horse's chances so much that I told *Toronto Sun* sports editor George Gross: "This colt could become the best three-year-old in North America. I know people might laugh at me, but in my opinion Native Guest could become another Secretariat."

Because Native Guest had not been nominated to the race through a series of sustaining payments, it cost $10,000 to supplement him to the race, which had a purse of $210,600. Native Guest had speed to burn, but he couldn't sustain it over the mile-and-three-sixteenths race and he faded to seventh by eleven and a half lengths to Master Derby, who had run fourth in the Kentucky Derby.

The Canadian Triple Crown was fast approaching, and I had been lined up to ride L'Enjoleur, the Winterbook favourite to win the Plate and highly touted to win the Kentucky Derby. His stock dropped on the U.S. Triple Crown front when he failed to win his first five starts, but he rebounded, winning the Quebec Derby by eight lengths, and he went into the Plate as the heavy favourite at slightly more than even odds. His main opponent was expected to be Greek Answer, who won one of the two divisions of the Plate Trial Stakes.

My return to Ontario for the Plate weekend prompted *Toronto Sun* columnist Trent Frayne to write: "Sandy Hawley is currently the world's hottest jockey. He is the rage of Hollywood Park out in California, more sought after than Raquel Welch, bigger even than Monty Hall. He is to jockeys what Telly Savalas is to cops."

The year before, when L'Enjoleur had won the Laurel Maturity — and back then it was one of the toughest races to win — his groom, Leo Davison, said that he was just an average horse until I got on him. I got after him a little bit with the whip — just woke him up — and he just started winning races after that. Going into the Queen's Plate, I knew I had a great chance to win it with him. Greek Answer led for the opening half mile in a blistering 45 3/5 seconds, but I was comfortably in second and we edged away and won by five and a half lengths. It was very thrilling to win the Plate for owner Jean-Louis Levesque, who had also bred the horse. He was probably one of Canada's top owners of all time. He was a wonderful guy and a great guy to win for. He was just a very intelligent man — that came through when you spoke with him. And he absolutely loved horse racing. What I remember most is that he always had a smile on his face. That, and he was always well dressed.

We returned to Hollywood Park and easily won the meet, recording twelve victories in the final four days to finish with 118 overall. *Toronto Sun* columnist Jim Coleman summed it up: "The California Gold Rush of 1849 didn't produce as much loot as Sandy extracted from the dusty racing strip of Hollywood Park in the past three months."

Bob Benoit:
He was very popular, and he was a publicity man's jewel because he'd never say no to anything. He'd do anything for you and go any place — radio, television, whatever — and present himself so well. He just stood out in that regard, just so much class. He gave the impression that we wanted to get across to the fans — and to those who might become fans and find an idol. He certainly fit that bill.

Marje Everett, in particular, played a significant role.

Gordon Jones:
Marje Everett loved nice people who were also glittering, special people, and she'd bring them into her Turf Club. Jack Lemmon, Walter Matthau, Mickey Rooney — they were there. You name athletes — Joe Namath, Chris Evert — and they were there. Her dear friend was Elizabeth Taylor. Cary Grant was there all the time. They were just generally a glittering selection of people.

Shoemaker was her favourite rider. Sandy wasn't around as long as Shoemaker, but Sandy was the kind of guy who, whenever he wanted to, would have found an open door to her directors' room up there, which people would die to be in. She ran that thing like Queen Elizabeth. She *was* Hollywood Park.

Marje Everett:
I was unusually close to many of the jockeys. I was very fortunate in knowing most of the fine boys and their integrity. We had a great personal relationship in most

cases, and that's how I knew Sherrie and some of the other wives.

In the industry, we marketed the jockeys, because they had the colour and they brought in the people and they had the following. It would be like taking some of the players in baseball or something, and the ones that were successful and colourful, you'd market them. In my case it was because I liked them so much. We were fortunate to attract such outstanding individuals. Sandy was a very attractive, well-respected person, wonderful disposition.

We returned home for the Woodbine meet, then I decided to cut back on my schedule, giving way to Braulio Baeza in the battle for top purse earnings. But I accepted the odd mount, including a trip back to Maryland in November to ride in the Washington D.C. International, one of the world's top grass races. The Texas oilman Nelson Bunker Hunt, who had one of the top breeding/racing operations in the world, hired me to ride Nobiliary, part of a solid coupled entry with the great Dahlia, one of the best mares of all time. Dahlia had won the Canadian International in 1974 with Lester Piggott, and I was excited about riding her in 1975 in the same race.

I didn't finish in the top three with Dahlia in the Canadian International. But after the race, in Bruce Walker's office, we met Maurice Zilber, the mare's trainer, and Nelson Bunker Hunt. Colin and I mentioned that we'd love to ride Dahlia in the D.C. International and they agreed. Colin and I flew down a couple of days before the race, and the overnight sheet, which indicates the races on the card and the jockeys who are named to ride the horses, showed that Lester Piggott would be riding Dahlia while we were on Nobiliary.

We're pretty upset about that. I didn't even know who Nobiliary was. We wondered what the heck was going on.

We looked at the *Daily Racing Form* to get a line on the horse's running style and past performances, and we realized that Nobiliary was always on the lead and was a bit of a rabbit — a horse deliberately sent out to set a fast pace for an entry mate. In this case, for Dahlia. We got the feeling we were being messed around with; it seemed to us like a bad deal because they'd known all along that Lester was going to ride Dahlia. Colin talked to Bruce Walker, who said, "Nobiliary is a nice filly. I think she's got a good shot in the race." We figured that we had given up our mounts at Woodbine, so we might as well stay in Maryland and ride Nobiliary.

We also talked to Maurice Zilber, and he said: "You know what? In England you can bet on horses separately, even if they're running together as an entry, and Nobiliary is a big price." He added: "I'm not betting on Dhalia. I'm betting on Nobiliary because I think she can win the race." That made me feel better about matters. Until the day of the race, when I walked into the paddock and said, "Mr. Zilber, what would you like me to do?" "I want you to go to the lead," he replied. And I thought to myself, "Oh, yeah, here we go. He's going to want me to go to the lead and set the pace for Dahlia."

Nobiliary was soaking wet — all lathered up — leading up to the starting gate because she was a very nervous horse. It turned out that one of the other horses had lost a shoe warming up, so they had to delay the race for about ten minutes. While the blacksmith changed this horse's shoe, all the riders got off their horses. By the time I got back on Nobiliary, she was all dried off. She must have just thought, "Hey, I was out here for a little workout, now I'm being cooled out." And she did — she cooled out. The delay was probably a blessing in disguise.

Now the race was on and I had to follow instructions. I came out of the starting gate and, within the first quarter mile I was on the lead, head and head with Angel Cordero. This was pretty early in my career, while Angel was an experienced hand. He didn't want himself to get killed off by getting caught up in a speed duel. "Take back, Sandy. Take back," he said.

"Angel," I responded, "I got instructions to go to the lead. I'm sorry, but I'm going to the lead."

So he took back because he didn't want to go head and head all the way; it was a long race. At the head of the stretch, I asked her to run — somebody was trying to squeeze through inside, but there was no room, and I couldn't believe no one was coming at that point. I asked my mount to run and she opened up and won by about three lengths. There was a claim of foul, but it was dismissed by the stewards. Dahlia didn't finish in the top three.

I finished the season third in wins with 312 — that was 156 behind Chris McCarron — and second in purse earnings with slightly more than $3.5 million, roughly $150,000 behind Braulio Baeza.

"The only thing that stopped Sandy Hawley in 1975 was the arrival of 1976," *Toronto Sun* columnist Trent Frayne wrote. On the last day of the old year he won a stakes race with a beast called Big Destiny, which could scarcely have been more appropriate. Ever since 1969, when he was the leading apprentice jockey on the Ontario circuit, Hawley's destiny had loomed larger than life-size."

Early in January, I was invested in the Order of Canada, which is awarded annually to Canadians in various fields for contributions to the country. I was there amongst scientists, doctors and lawyers and people of that ilk and stature, and I found myself wondering, "What am I doing here? All I did was win a few races." Around the same time, I was also named as the winner of the George Woolf Award for contributions to racing. I was up for the award along with Ron Turcotte, Bill Mahorney, Frank Olivares and Darrel McHargue. It was overwhelming, since I hadn't ridden in California for that long.

There was tremendous excitement and anticipation when I returned to California and renewed my competitive battle with Laffit Pincay. I finished ahead of him at the Santa Anita meet, snapping his streak of five consecutive titles. I also broke Bill Shoemaker's record for money won at the meet, highlighted by a win aboard One on the Aisle in the San Juan Capistrano Handicap. I was leading North America in victories heading into the Hollywood Park meet, and Laffit and I engaged in a tremendous battle that came right down to the end. He was suspended for ten days for a riding infraction during the Hollywood meet, and I led by twenty-seven wins at one point, but he overtook me on the final day and finished ahead, 125–122. Hollywood Park gave us both commemorative trophies. Before his suspension began, Laffit switched agents, going from Vince DeGregory to George O'Bryan, who had been working for Don Pierce.

Laffit Pincay:
When I came back, I had a talk with my agent. I said, "Listen, I just want you to do me a favour. I'll do my job, and you do your job. I'm going to leave you alone, you leave me alone. I'm going to try hard again; let's just concentrate and do good."

I'm telling you, I started working very, very hard, and we started winning a lot of races. The combination clicked, and pretty soon I was in a position of being close to Sandy and then winning.

I'm very proud of myself, because to me, Sandy was the best rider in the country. It was an accomplishment I'm still very proud of. It was such a great meeting for both of us. I thought it was very nice that they gave both of us a trophy — anybody could have won. A lot of guys were betting that I would win, and some were betting that Sandy would win. The betting started when I got to be about ten winners behind and the newspapers got into it. It was really good for racing in California.

Laffit and I had some very competitive seasons, but it was an honour to ride against him and a pleasure to be his friend. While it's every man for himself when you're on the racetrack, Laffit was the first to give you a break when you were in trouble. He was generous when he saw you were in a bad spot.

In June 1976 I came to Woodbine to ride in the Plate Trial Stakes, but finished second with Laissez Passer in one division and second in the other with Le Gaspesien. Both horses were owned by Jean-Louis Levesque. I picked Laissez Passer to ride in the Plate, and placed fourth to the 8–5 favourite, Norcliffe, who had won the Plate Trial division in which I rode Le Gaspesien. The winning jockey was Jeff Fell, who'd captured Canada's riding crown the year before, at age nineteen, after finishing as the top apprentice in the country in 1974. Jeff appeared to be the next Canadian to go to the U.S. to showcase his skills.

In the Canadian International in October, I had the mount on Youth, another star turf horse owned by Nelson Bunker Hunt and trained by Maurice Zilber. Youth was a three-year-old colt who was being touted as the "second Secretariat." He came into the race with five wins in seven starts on the season. He'd also won the French Derby in June, and he and stablemate Empery, the English Derby winner, had been jointly syndicated for $12 million. He came to Canada off a third-place finish in the Prix de l'Arc de Triomphe, Europe's most prestigious grass race, and went postward at less than even money.

Youth was a big, strong three-year-old. In Europe, the trainers like you to keep horses covered up — that means they like you to stay behind other horses, because as soon as they see daylight, they want to go. I had a hard time keeping him in behind other horses — he was a little bit green, being only a three-year-old — but boy, when I let him go, he exploded and won by four easy lengths. In the words of the *Daily Racing Form*, Youth "drew away to win as the rider pleased." After the race, I said, "He's just a super horse. He's the best horse I've ever ridden."

Less than a week later, I surpassed the $4 million mark in purses, becoming only the third rider in history to do so. With almost a full two months left in the season, I had a shot at breaking Laffit Pincay's world record of $4,251,060. Just to be in the running was a tremendous thrill, but my focus was on Youth — and winning the D.C. International again. Youth was one of the favourites going into the race. I was supposed to go out and work him one morning, but neither Mr. Hunt nor Mr. Zilber was there. It was around nine o'clock. They had said they wanted me to work the horse around that time, so the groom had him ready with the tack on and we were all set to go. Mr. Zilber's travelling stablehands suggested I just go ahead and work Youth before the turf training closed. I think I only worked him about half a mile, and he went very easily. As soon as I came back, Hunt and Zilber drove up and Mr. Zilber said, "Okay, you can take him out and work him now."

"Well, we already worked him," I replied. "We went half a mile." He told me to take him back out again; they wanted to see him go. So, I took him back out again and worked him another half a mile. I knew that they train differently in Europe than we do here in North America, but I was shocked that Mr. Zilber wanted me to take the horse back out and work him again.

But Youth was just an amazing horse. A day or so before the race, he had a little bit of swelling in his ankle, and Maurice Zilber, who was a bit of a character, said, "I may have to scratch him because of his ankle." I was a bit concerned, so I asked him: "Mr. Zilber, is he going to race tomorrow?"

"Don't worry, Sandy," he said. "He's better than he was in the Canadian International. We'll win by the length of the stretch." Youth did have a bit of swelling in his leg, but Mr. Zilber was playing dumb about it with the press.

Coming out of the gate and going down the backstretch for the first time, I was trying to keep him covered up behind the first group of horses. But as we came around the first turn for the first time, a jockey from Hong Kong came straight up in front of me and shut me off. I had to stand right up, and now I was two flights behind the leaders. A little gap opened up, and I wanted to move up and join the leaders because we were nearing the halfway point in the race. I didn't even ask Youth to run; I just gave him a little urging, and he shot right through the hole.

I had to take hold of him again in the final turn because we were in behind the leaders. I just wheeled him to the outside after the final turn and let him go; he drifted in a little bit with me because, as I mentioned, he was a little bit green. But he ended up winning by about ten lengths. There was an inquiry from the rider of On My Way Too, but the stewards rejected it.

Elizabeth Taylor was in the winner's circle to help with the presentation — I actually have that picture — and she gave me a kiss on the cheek. That was pretty cool, to say the least. I would later meet her again, through Hollywood Park vice chairman Marje Everett.

Colin came up with the idea of going to New York in hopes of winning enough money to finish the season first overall in wins and purse earnings — and, hopefully, give me a shot at the Eclipse Award as the top rider in North America. The purses were so much better in New York than in Ontario. Less than a week later, at Aqueduct, I eclipsed the existing world record in purse earnings, guiding Moonlight Jig to victory in a claiming race. My fellow riders kidded me, calling me Moneybags and Millionaire.

We had one more goal on the season — to reach the 3,000-win mark and do it at home. I needed thirty-eight wins with roughly a month left in the Ontario racing season. On December 4, we accomplished the goal on a snowy Saturday afternoon at Greenwood, guiding the aptly named filly Glad to Be to a smashing seven-length victory. The winning trainer was Bob Tiller. Coincidentally, when I recorded my 6,000th career win, it was with another Tiller-trained horse, Summer Commander, and it also happened at Greenwood.

Based on what Colin and I achieved in 1976, we thought it would be hard for the voters not to give us the Eclipse Award that had eluded us in the 500-win season of 1973. But you can't control those things; you can only do your best. After I notched my 3,000th career winner, I decided to shut down my season and take a break, more or less conceding the earnings title to Angel Cordero Jr. He finished with a world-record $4,709,500, almost $170,000 more than me, but I finished first in wins with 413, twenty-seven ahead of Laffit Pincay, who also decided to take an early vacation. Angel Cordero had 139 fewer winners than me.

The voting for the Eclipse was completed before the season had ended, and I was named the top jockey. We'd had another great year, and it was an honour to be recognized with the award.

In addition, I received the Lou Marsh Trophy — for the second time — as the top athlete in Canada as voted by the Canadian media. It was doubly nice to win it in tandem with the Eclipse Award. It really capped off a satisfying season.

CHAPTER SIX

Coming to an End
in Canada

The Ontario Jockey Club's 1977 media guide posed an interesting question about me: "Is there anything left for jockey Sandy Hawley to accomplish in thoroughbred racing?" Well, it turned out there was. Lots.

We decided to take some time off and did not begin riding until mid-February, when we picked up where we'd left off in California. A few months later I picked up the mount on Run Dusty Run for the Belmont Stakes. This was the year in which Seattle Slew was trying to sweep the Triple Crown, having won the Kentucky Derby and Preakness Stakes. Darrel McHargue had ridden Run Dusty Run to a second-place finish in the Derby and third place in the Preakness. In the Belmont, I finished second to Seattle Slew, who lost only one start in seven races that season after winning all three of his starts as a two-year-old.

Jean Cruguet, a native of France who rode regularly in New York, was aboard Seattle Slew for his historic sweep. He came to Woodbine the day after the Belmont to ride Jean-Louis Levesque's Giboulee in the Plate Trial Stakes. I had finished fifth with the colt in the Peter Pan Stakes at Belmont, but I could not commit to the Plate Trial because of a previous call to ride another horse in California the same day. Giboulee won the Plate Trial Stakes, and it was decided that Cruguet would ride him in the Queen's Plate. The problem was that Colin claimed he had been given a verbal commitment by Mr. Levesque's son, Pierre, to let me ride Giboulee in the Plate. He lodged a complaint with the Ontario Racing Commission stewards, who ordered Colin and Pierre to work it out between themselves. In the end, Jean Cruguet maintained the mount, and I ended up without one for only the second time since I'd begun regularly competing in the race in 1970. In the Plate,

Giboulee finished third, by four lengths, to Sound Reason, the 3–2 race favourite.

I missed a scheduled return to California to ride in the Del Mar Futurity when the U.S. customs officials at Toronto International Airport refused me entry because my American work permit had not been renewed — even though the papers had been signed a month before. Coincidentally, Bob Benoit, Hollywood Park's vice president of administration and the person who signed the work-permit papers, happened to be visiting Woodbine, and the situation was rectified a few days later. In my absence, the horse I was scheduled to ride did not run well.

The Canadian International Championship Stakes loomed on the fall racing calendar, and we had to choose between Majestic Light, owned by Ogden Mills (Dinny) Phipps, and Exceller, owned by Nelson Bunker Hunt. Majestic Light had been one of the top grass horses in the U.S., while Exceller had been one of the best on turf in Europe.

"It's a terrible predicament for a man to find himself in, like trying to choose between Sophia Loren and Raquel Welch, both of them clawing at you," wrote *Toronto Sun* columnist Trent Frayne. "It's like deciding between the beef Wellington and the lobster tails steamed in white Portuguese port. It's like wondering if you should take the Ferrari and wear your Gucci boots, or the Rolls Royce and your crocodile loafers. I mean, it's a hell of a situation for a boy who hangs his hat in Mississauga."

We had done so well over the past two years with horses trained by Maurice Zilber and owned by Hunt. But 1977 just happened to be the year that I had won with Majestic Light in a couple of big turf races — including a victory over Exceller in a race in New York. We didn't know which would be the better horse, but Colin and I felt we had more opportunities with Mr. Phipps. And in any event, it's hard to take off a winning horse.

Exceller was coupled with Diagramatic, who was also owned by Mr. Hunt, and they went postward as the 6–5 favourite, while Majestic Light was second choice at just under 7–5. Angel Cordero Jr. was on Exceller, and he rallied from off the pace to beat my horse by a length. I had a one-length lead at the top of the stretch, and actually widened that advantage, but Exceller caught my horse within the final furlong.

Exceller and Majestic Light also battled one another in the D.C. International in Maryland, and this time Johnny D., who had run third in the Canadian International, won. Johnny D., ridden by teenage sensation Steve Cauthen, got out to an early lead and held it; I finished second with Majestic Light, while Cordero ran third with Exceller. There was criticism in the papers the next day that Angel and I had been watching one another too much and forgotten about Johnny D. But Johnny D. was a nice horse, and he went on to beat us again in the Turf Classic Stakes in New York by three and a half lengths. He got on the lead again this time, and I trailed him by only a head with a quarter mile to the wire, but he drew away. Exceller ran a distant seventh in the field of nine. Johnny D.'s win in the Turf Classic actually made Cordero and me look a little better, because he justified his ability. All three horses were tough.

I finished the season with 263 wins, eighth overall behind Steve Cauthen, who registered 487 wins and set a world purse-earnings record with a whopping $6,151,750, about $1.4 million more than Cordero's one-year-old record. I placed sixth with $3,537,422. Steve Cauthen was a seventeen-year-old from Kentucky, and of course he became known as The Kid. He was a tremendous rider; I couldn't believe how polished he was right from the very beginning. He'd only ridden a few races, but he already looked like a journeyman. It was amazing how poised he looked on a horse, but he was brought up around horses, so he had a bit of a head start. Not only was he unusually polished for a young rider, but he also had a good head on his shoulders. He was very articulate and handed himself very well with the media. He was a great credit to horse racing.

Cauthen would go on to sweep the U.S. Triple Crown the following year with Affirmed. While 1978 would be a highlight year for him, it represented a turning point of sorts for me in many ways. My marriage to Sherrie was starting to fall apart. She was busy with her show horses and was doing well, winning a lot of competitions and at one point grooming Marje

Everett's Stardust Mel, a one-time star thoroughbred who had been converted into a show jumper and was ridden at major North American tournaments by Ian Millar of Canada's Olympic equestrian team. Meanwhile, I was riding at tracks all over the place. In a nutshell, I felt as though we had grown apart. She had her friends and I had mine.

Sherrie Hawley:
I was very successful. Maybe I did do the horse-show business a bit too much, I don't know. I look back, and everything with him was good. He was always a gentleman. He never brought any bad stuff to the races or to his profession. He always conducted himself in a gentlemanly manner. I just look back on my life with him as a great time, and I'd do it all again, given the chance. I don't for a minute regret any of it, even the way it turned out.

It was hard getting divorced from Sandy, because his nickname around the track was God. That's what they used to call him. I tried to make my living in the horse-show business because I was too ashamed to go back to the track, so to speak, because I was divorced from Sandy Hawley. He had such a great reputation it was kind of hard to hold your head up after that. But when I finally went back, people didn't care; they just accepted me.

I was running into snags on the business side, too. There were some income-tax problems that made it difficult for me to ride regularly in the winter and spring in California. As a non-resident, I was subject to a 76 per cent tax bite from the U.S. government. Late in the fall of 1977, my business manager, Roger Smith, started trying to resolve matters. He claimed that, according to the tax treaty between Canada and the United States, I was being discriminated against in America because I was a Canadian. While Roger pursued my case, I rode at Santa Anita in late December and into the early stages of the new year.

Bobby Frankel was hopeful that I could stay in California. I was riding a lot of horses for him, and for a lot of other top trainers, too, but it was very frustrating that I was paying that much income tax. I really wasn't making any money by staying there; from a personal-finance perspective, I could do better riding in Canada. So, that's what I decided to do; I spent most of the year north of the border.

In time, we finally got things settled when I became a resident alien; that cut down on my taxes quite a bit. Another option would have been to become a U.S. citizen. But it was a tough enough decision to become a resident, which required me to spend at least six months a year in the States. Canada was my home, and I was proud to be a Canadian — and I still am.

As noted, I returned home to ride full time in Ontario during the spring meet, flying back to California for the occasional big race. My string of five consecutive victories in the Canadian Oaks ended when I finished second, with L'Alezane, to entry mate La Voyageuse. On a happier note, I rode in the Queen's Plate again — and I won it, with Regal Embrace. That was probably my biggest thrill at Woodbine and in Canada. The horse was bred and owned by E.P. Taylor, who owned and operated Windfields Farm, the place where my horse-racing journey had begun when it was known as the National Stud Farm. Only twelve years later I was standing in the winner's circle, not only winning the biggest race in Canada, but standing alongside the great E.P. Taylor himself, as well as his lovely wife. Mr. Taylor was a pioneer who more or less made racing what it is today in Canada. It was a real privilege to win the Plate for him.

Regal Embrace was not the soundest horse in the world, and trainer Mac Benson did a tremendous job of having him perfect for that race. He told me that if no one wanted the lead, I should go ahead and take it if it was an easy lead. That's what happened after we got around the first turn. Coming around the final turn, I still had a lot of horse under me. I looked over my shoulder and nobody was coming. Once I got about three-quarters of the way around the turn, and before I hit the head of the stretch, I thought, "I'm going to ask him for everything he's got right now; I'm not going to wait for another horse to come to me, because I know Overskate is going to be flying." Overskate was the big favourite after winning the Plate Trial Stakes. Partway around the turn, I just let Regal Embrace go full tilt and thought, "Let's try to open up as far as we can and see if we can get to the wire first." We won by a neck in a time of two minutes and two seconds, tying Victoria Park's stakes record set in 1960. Had Overskate won the race, it would have given Robin Platts a record fifth Plate winner.

I leapt out of the irons, similar to the way I had when I won the Plate in '71 with Kennedy Road. It was the dismount made famous in Ontario by my one of my idols, Avelino Gomez, whom I had just tied for Plate victories with four. When you win a race like the Plate, it makes you leap even higher. It was Mr. Taylor's tenth win at the Queen's Plate, but only the first since Northern Dancer's historic victory fourteen years before. It was the first Plate win for Mac Benson, an American who had recently taken over as Windfields' trainer. Regal Embrace hadn't raced as a two-year-old because he was big and gangly and had problems with his ankles. Prior to the Plate, he'd been in only five races, winning four, none of them stakes races.

Overskate went on to win the other two legs of the Canadian Triple Crown, en route to winning the Canadian horse-of-the-year title, which he won again the following year. Regal Embrace never repeated his Plate success because of soundness issues, but he won the most important race of his life.

It would also be the last time I won the Plate, although not for a lack of trying in later years.

* * *

Around this time, the racing world was shocked and saddened by a racing tragedy in New York. On July 13, Ron Turcotte, who had done so well in Ontario in the early '60s and then achieved greatness in the U.S. with the likes of back-to-back Kentucky Derby winners Riva Ridge in 1972 and Secretariat in 1973, was permanently disabled after a racing spill. Jeff Fell, who led the Ontario circuit from 1975 through 1977 and had graduated to become one of the top riders on the tough New

York circuit, was involved in the awful mishap. Fifty yards out of the starting gate, Jeff's mount drifted into the path of Turcotte, whose mount clipped heels with another horse and fell down, flinging Ron, as if from a slingshot, out of the saddle. He landed hard on his back and was paralyzed below the waist.

When you watch horses bursting out of the starting gate, it often looks chaotic. Riders are jockeying for position, and I'm sure that's what Jeff Fell was doing. It was just a sad, unfortunate situation. I'd crossed paths with Ron when I rode the odd time in New York, but I got to know him really well when we both rode in that competition in South Africa. We've become good friends. He was a character, a great jockey and just a super-nice guy. I don't know of anyone who ever had anything bad to say about Ron Turcotte. A number of times since then, I've had fun chatting with him. He would come to the Queen's Plate every year, and I'd see him at various other functions. He rode for seventeen years and won 3,032 races, earning a reputation as one of the best and toughest riders ever to sit on a horse.

* * *

In October, some fans started pelting me with foul language after I failed to win on some heavy favourites on back-to-back days. I also went through a slump in the Greenwood meet, riding only one winner in my first twenty-three mounts, many of which were favourites. You sometimes go through a spell where you're just not winning, where the horses are just not running up to expectations. Steve Cauthen went through a run of 110 consecutive races without a winner. Despite the dry spell, I wasn't about to change my style; I was determined to keep doing the things that had made me so successful, and hope I could ride out the storm. Fans would holler and scream and get pretty obnoxious. I didn't let it get to me, but when they started getting obnoxious when there were kids around, it bothered me — they shouldn't have to hear that bad language. I told track security that they should handle the situation, not for my sake but for the young kids who were around.

I don't remember what year it was, but there was one time when somebody called backstretch security and said, "I'm coming to the racetrack today and I have a high-powered rifle with me, and I'm going to shoot Sandy Hawley." When I came to the jocks' room that morning, they told me about the threat. I said, "If I don't ride today, the guy's just going to come back tomorrow and do the same thing, so I'm going to go ahead and ride." You can't let someone like that stop you. There was a heavy security presence watching out for me, but I went ahead and rode without incident. Still, it was tense. I was in the post parade before one race, and I was kind of leaning back, as if to hide behind Albert Trudell, the pony boy. He asked me why I was leaning back, and I told him there was a guy who had threatened to come to the races with a high-powered rifle. I think he kind of got a little excited about that; thought I was trying to hide behind him. So he made a bit of a joke about it, but at the same time it was pretty serious.

I don't remember making any big swoops around the outside that day; I stayed on the inside all day. We used to have a tram that took us from the racetrack back to the jockeys' room, and I had two security guards sitting beside me every time I went back on the wagon.

I won another Canadian title that year, as well as my first Sovereign Award. Introduced in 1975, this was the Canadian equivalent of the Eclipse Award. I placed third in the continent in wins, with 360 from 1,338 mounts. Eddie Delahoussaye led with 384 from 1,666 mounts, while Darrel McHargue placed second with 375 from 1,762. McHargue won the money title with $6,188,353, while I placed twelfth with $2,877,920.

The end of the Woodbine autumn meet in October 1978 drew to a close my full-time career in Canada. My new status as a resident alien meant that I had to focus on riding in the United States. Just a few months later, in May 1979, I would ride in the Kentucky Derby, the most famous of American races, for the first time, with a horse called Golden Act.

CHAPTER SEVEN

The U.S. Years

Golden Act had won the Louisiana Derby and then the Arkansas Derby, a major tune-up for the Kentucky Derby. I had hurt my ankle in a starting gate mishap at Santa Anita, and it was pretty bruised up and swollen. Dr. Robert Kerlan, the California-based orthopedist who did some amazing work on an ankle I'd banged up a few years before, worked his magic on me again, freezing my ankle so that I could ride in the Arkansas Derby. Going into the Kentucky Derby, we were rated at about 10–1. The buzz centred around Spectacular Bid, the reigning North American two-year-old champion who had won the Florida Derby and the Blue Grass Stakes in preparation for the Kentucky Derby.

On Kentucky Derby day, I was probably the most nervous I'd ever been. There way an old saying: "You have a nervous pee before you go out." I remember going into the bathroom for a pee — and nothing would come out. Then, walking away from the bathroom, it felt like I had to go again. That really illustrates what the saying meant. I was still nervous when I went into the paddock to get my instructions from trainer Loren Rettele, but I could take some solace in the fact I wasn't riding one of the favourites. I can only imagine what Ronnie Franklin went through, having to ride Spectacular Bid.

Golden Act was the type of horse who had to wake up in a race. He was a little bit lazy, but once he woke up he started flying. He was just like that in the Derby. He had a really good trip, but it's tough to come from so far back in the Kentucky Derby because there are so many horses in the field. He ran a really good race, but Spectacular Bid, the 3–5 favourite, was just a little too good that day — he won by two and a half lengths. We finished third by five and a half, and there was no disgrace in that. Spectacular Bid was a monster horse.

Golden Act did well enough to encourage the horse's trainer and owners to go forward to the Preakness Stakes. It was a real pleasure to go back to Maryland, where I had ridden for a couple of years earlier in my career, and renew acquaintances with some of my old buddies. It was even more special because I actually had a shot at winning the race. But again, Spectacular Bid was just too good, and we finished second by five and a half lengths.

I was so proud of the way Golden Act, who was just an average-sized horse, had run so well against Spectacular Bid in these two major races. He was one of my favourite horses of all time — he tried so hard. And I was happy to go forward with Golden Act and try to beat the Bid in the Belmont Stakes and spoil his chance of sweeping the Triple Crown. At a mile and a half, the Belmont is the longest of the three races, which was to our advantage. As nice as it is to see a Triple Crown winner, when you're in a race, you're still trying to beat the son of a gun.

Spectacular Bid didn't win the Belmont — he ran third — but we didn't win, either. We finished second. Coastal, who hadn't run in the first two legs of the Triple Crown, won the race. It would have been great to be the one to beat a superhorse like Spectacular Bid; nobody ever remembers who finished second — except me, perhaps, and Golden Act's connections.

I returned to Woodbine for the major summer races, and things started off well when we won the Oaks — my sixth victory in the race — with Bahnam Yousif's Kamar. I came into the Plate with E.P. Taylor's Bold Agent, with whom I won a division of the Plate Trial Stakes. Steady Growth, owned by Bud Willmot, won the other division with Brian Swatuk. Trainer John Tammaro touted Steady Growth as the best three-year-old colt in the country, but he wanted to withdraw the horse from the race after rain left the track sloppy. Mr. Willmot, whose Kinghaven Farms was becoming one of the stronger breeding/racing operations in the country, opted to race Steady Growth. We were the 7–10 favourite because of a coupling with entry mate Bridle Path, but we never seriously threatened Steady Growth, who prevailed by two and a half lengths. I think the track conditions were against Bold Agent; he never really got his footing at all, just couldn't get any traction. He wasn't himself in that race, but Steady Growth proved to be no slouch, going on to the U.S. and doing well.

On the July 1 holiday weekend, I won only one of seven races, and the bettors, who were not in a forgiving mood, gave me an earful. That prompted veteran racing writer Jim Coleman to come to my defence in his column.

> The unseemly demonstration by the boo birds at Woodbine merely confirmed a widely held belief that there are countless tinhorn would-be gamblers who, before entering a racetrack, leave their pea-sized brains in the parking lot.
>
> Seldom, if ever, in the history of thoroughbred racing has there been another jockey who equalled Sandy Hawley's standard of consistent riding success, equestrian intelligence and instinctive gentlemanly deportment. Those twits who booed Hawley should confine themselves to buying bingo cards or lottery tickets.

I rode Bold Agent in the Prince of Wales Stakes, finishing third. Steady Growth didn't win, either, placing second as Mass Rally recorded an upset. He was ridden by George Ho Sang for owner Dave Mann and trainer Donnie Campbell — the son of Duke Campbell, who had played such a pivotal role early in my career. I won the Breeders' Stakes with Bridle Path, who was coupled with Bold Agent in the Plate because both were owned by E.P. Taylor. Bridle Path was an offspring of Kennedy Road, whom I had ridden to victory in the 1971 Queen's Plate.

A little later in the year, I went to France to ride in the Prix de l'Arc de Triomphe, Europe's premier distance grass race. I was hired to ride Telescopio, owned by Bahnam Yousif and Ahmed Foustok. It was a tremendous experience, but since it was the first time I'd ridden in France, I had to adjust to some differences in racing style. In France, they run clockwise — as opposed to counter-clockwise in North America — and one of the Woodbine valets warned me that they run a little rougher in France than they do in North America. I arrived ten days before the Arc, and Telescopio won a prep race for it by about eight lengths — he demolished the competition — but he beat a very average field.

Colin Wick:
I was in the owner's box with Mr. Foustok and his trainer, Maurice Zilber. I was in the paddock when Maurice said to Sandy, "They don't go right away in the beginning. You've got to watch a horse that Yves Saint-Martin is riding, which is the favourite. Just take in behind him and let him make the pace, and when the time is right, you go."

So, now I went into the box with Mr. Zilber and Mr. Foustok, and the race started. It's a mile and a quarter. Sandy is two in front. Maurice told Mr. Foustok, "I gave him specific orders to stay in behind Yves Saint-Martin." Half a mile into the race, Yves Saint-Martin came alongside Sandy, ready to take over, and Sandy opened up another length. As the race went on, Maurice said to Mr. Foustok, "The American riders, they don't understand when you give them instructions." I think he was looking for an excuse if the horse got beat.

As they turned for home, Sandy opened up four. Yves Saint-Martin was chasing him now. By the end of the race, he had won by several lengths. I remember Maurice Zilber saying to Mr. Foustok, "That's why I brought Sandy Hawley in: one of the greatest riders in the world!"

Mr. Foustok offered me a contract, involving a significant six-figure retainer, to ride first call for him in France, where he had a large stable. I had concerns about the language barrier; I was also first or second in California at the time, and I'd kind of made it my second home after Canada. When I think about it now, maybe I should have gone just for the experience — to broaden my horizons. But at the time, with things going so well in the States, declining the offer seemed the best decision.

I heard that Mr. Foustok didn't have that good of a year. As for Telescopio, he didn't fare all that well in the Arc.

* * *

On a personal note, in 1979 I met a woman named Vicki Grohs who would become my second wife. Vicki worked at a concession stand at Santa Anita, and we met at an awards ceremony in Las Vegas. Vicki's father, Phil, was a jockey who had been killed in a racing accident before my riding career began. He rode mostly in northern California, occasionally in southern California. Vicki was only seven or eight when he died. Over the course of the next few months the relationship became serious, although I still wasn't divorced from Sherrie and hadn't really considered remarrying.

I finished the year ninth in purses won with $4,043,307, just under half of the haul amassed by Laffit Pincay Jr., who established a world record with $8,183,535. I recorded 214 victories, which placed me in the top twenty-five in the continent, but I rode in only 1,086 races, one of my lowest since I'd begun riding full time in 1969.

Of all my years in racing, 1980 may have been the most difficult, both personally and professionally. Colin decided that year that he wanted to come home rather than continue living in California. That meant I would have to choose between pressing on without him or returning to Canada and continuing our association. It was a very, very tough decision. I had so many California trainers telling me that I should stay. There was more money to be made in California, better horses to ride, and more opportunities to ride in big races. I tried to talk Colin into staying on as my agent, but his wife Margaret lived in Canada and didn't want to move to California. I could understand his situation perfectly. He loved to fish, and he owned a cottage north of North Bay — which he still owns, in fact — that he loved.

Colin Wick:
I was starting to get tired of living in hotels. He was like my son and I was like his father, but I had to make a

decision. I told him, "I've either got to move out here and make it my home or I've got to go home."

I didn't just leave on the spur of the moment; I'd looked around to find an agent for him that he'd be happy with before I left. It was like three months before I left.

Gary Jones:
He was a great agent; he was like Sandy's daddy. If Sandy would get down in the lip, Wicksey would go in there and just ream him and Sandy would come out the next day and ride like a son-of-a-gun. It was a really strange relationship. Wicksey was very much a key to his confidence.

It was very tough on me when Colin went back home, because we'd been together my whole career. But my business was good in California, so I decided to stay there year-round. Getting used to a new agent wasn't the only problem I had — I also had income-tax problems to deal with, and I had to use money from my registered retirement savings plan to settle accounts. A newspaper story came out around that time suggesting that I might have gone broke. I wasn't broke, but paying the back taxes cost me a big chunk.

Business wasn't going too well with my new agent, meanwhile, and it didn't help when I suffered a couple of injuries. I wrenched an ankle in a racing accident, then I suffered a freak mishap at home: the phone rang and I got up to answer it and felt something sharp go into my foot. I looked at the sole of my foot and couldn't see anything, but at the same time I couldn't bend my toe. I saw Dr. Robert Kerlan, the orthopedic specialist who had helped me several times in my career. I told him I thought I had stepped on a needle or something. And that was indeed the case: the eye end (rather than the point) of a sewing needle had got lodged in a bone in my toe where it bends and broken off. You could actually see it on the x-ray. I had to undergo surgery to remove it, so I missed another couple of weeks. In all, I missed some twenty-five days of racing because of the two injuries.

In June, I returned to Woodbine to ride in the Canadian Oaks, the race where I had enjoyed so much success in the past. But this time, the race was marred by tragedy: Avelino Gomez, one of my racing idols, was involved in a fatal mishap. His mount, Swisskin, owned by Helen Kasper, broke her right hind leg, triggering a three-horse spill. The incident happened along the backstretch, about half a mile from the wire, and it forced everyone behind — including me, aboard Middlemarch — to pull to the outside to avoid the spill.

When I finished the race, I saw Avelino in the ambulance. He looked like he was in a lot of pain, but he was talking, so it looked as though he was going to be okay. I was sure hoping he would. After the last race, Mickey Gomez, who booked the mounts for his brother, came back into the jockeys' room. I asked him how Avelino was, and he replied, "He has a few bumps and bruises, but he's probably going to be okay. He's just going to be off for a while."

I went out to dinner that night with Bruce Walker, the Ontario Jockey Club's publicity director, and my mom and dad. We had just finished dinner and were being served dessert when Bruce was called to the telephone. When he returned, he told us that Avelino had died on the operating table. It came as a complete shock. I could not believe the news, especially after talking to Mickey. But Avelino had suffered massive internal injuries.

The next day, reporters came to the track to interview me. About halfway through a television interview, I broke down and couldn't continue because I was overcome with feelings of despair. I had been very close to Avelino. I admired him because he was a tough competitor. He definitely wasn't your friend when he was on the racetrack, but in the jocks' room he was wonderful. I had a lot of respect for him and we got along well.

I was supposed to fly back to California, but I cancelled my flight because the Gomez family asked me to be a pallbearer. It was an honour I couldn't refuse. The other pallbearers were Brian Swatuk, George Ho Sang, Hugo Dittfach, Lloyd Duffy and Tom Hinojosa. The funeral was a very emotional event. Not only did I lose a good friend, but Canada had lost the best jockey it has ever had. His death still weighed heavily on my mind when I went back to California, and of course the riders there wanted to know what had happened. This was in the days before races were televised to other tracks via satellite for simulcast wagering. Guys such as Bill Shoemaker and Don Pierce had known Avelino from riding against him in Florida, and they were upset about his passing.

* * *

After some initial struggles, my business started to pick up in California with Harry (The Hat) Hacek as my agent. By midsummer, things really started to roll. Harry was working for a lot of the leading jockeys when he took my book, but he was a fly-by-night kind of guy. He'd be your agent one day, and then suddenly you'd be looking in vain for him — he'd disappear for months and then suddenly show up one day in New York. In the meantime, you'd have to find another agent. He did this not only to me, but to a number of other riders. Maybe that's how he got the name The Hat: because you'd never know where he was going to hang his hat.

I was fast approaching the 4,000th win of my career during this time. At first, I declined offers to come home to record the historic milestone because I worried that the time away from California would hurt my business. But eventually I changed my mind. On September 1, I reached 4,000 with a horse called Noble Martha. The crowd of 14,612 gave me a heartwarming salute. It was a tremendous thrill to get my 4000th win at home with my whole family there. I was greeted in the winner's circle by my mother and father; Vicki, who was my fiancée by then and had accompanied me on the trip; trainer Frank Merrill; my longtime mentor, Duke Campbell; Colin Wick; and Bruce Walker. There was also a fan nearby carrying a huge sign and wearing a Mexican sombrero, which he gave to me. I ended up wearing the hat in the picture taken in the winner's circle. Whoever that gentleman was, he loved me and always gave me good wishes any time I went on the track with a horse.

I became the eleventh rider in racing history to reach 4,000, but I had reached the plateau faster than any of the others. I finished the season with 219 wins from 1,278 mounts and rolled up $3,580,710 in purse earnings. Neither figured in the top ten, but given the injuries and the change of agents, it wasn't too bad of a year.

* * *

In May 1981, I rode in the Kentucky Derby again, this time with a horse called Partez, who was trained by Darrell Wayne Lukas. He was a former quarter-horse trainer who would become the top money-winning trainer in thoroughbred history, operating various stables throughout the United States and becoming a major player in the U.S. Triple Crown and the Breeders' Cup shortly after it started in 1984. Lukas, who would become better known simply as D. Wayne, trained Partez for the partnership of Greene and Davis. Partez was one of twenty-one horses in a crowded field that required nine horses to be grouped together in a mutuel field because the tote board at Churchill Downs could only accommodate twelve betting interests. Partez was joined in the mutuel field, which gave bettors nine horses for the price of one.

I rallied from more than six lengths back after three-quarters of a mile and reached the front in the early stretch. Now, this is the Kentucky Derby, the race every jockey wants to win, and your adrenaline is definitely rising at this point. You wish the wire would get there in a hurry, but unfortunately it didn't. Race favourite Pleasant Colony passed me and went on to win by three quarters of a length. With about seventy yards to go, I stood up, thinking we had already passed the wire. Woodchopper, who was behind me, finished three quarters of a length in front of my horse.

I had misjudged the finish line. It didn't cost my horse the race, and he would have been hard pressed to finish second anyway, but it was a mistake. I was not the first jockey to make it. Bill Shoemaker did it in 1957, and it cost him the win aboard Gallant Man, who lost by a nose to Iron Liege.

Partez's owners were understanding, and they let me ride the horse in the Preakness. It was great of them to do that. Once again, I made a strong move with my mount from far back but could only manage fifth this time, beaten by ten and a half lengths by Pleasant Colony. That was all for my horse in the Triple Crown. Pleasant Colony, meanwhile, failed to sweep the series, finishing third to Summing in the Belmont Stakes.

I returned to Woodbine in June to ride heavy favourite Rosy Briar in the Canadian Oaks. I finished out of the money and the fans started cursing and swearing. When you get beat on the favourite, you expect the fans to be angry, maybe do some yelling, but this was unusual for a Woodbine crowd. It was more in tune with what I'd expect from the New York fans. The abuse just shocked me.

I finished tenth on the continent in purse earnings, with just under $5 million — a personal best — although my 210 victories barely qualified for the top twenty-five in North America. I had won nineteen stakes races, which accounted for a lot of the money. In 1982, I placed twelfth in purse earnings with slightly more than $4 million, but my 176 wins didn't register in the top twenty-five.

The competition for quality mounts became even more fierce around this time as the likes of Chris McCarron, Gary Stevens, Ray Sibille and Eddie Delahoussaye came west. Meanwhile, because I was returning to Canada a few times each summer, some of the trainers from California were getting upset. Bobby Frankel was one of them, and he didn't put me on as many horses as he had when Colin Wick was booking my mounts. Business started tailing off with people getting kind of sour with me. So, I just asked Colin to come back and try and get me going again.

Colin came to me at one point and said, "Some of these trainers are saying you're on drugs." Maybe that was just an excuse for not putting me on their horses at the time, but I got very upset when I heard it because it wasn't true. I don't know why they would think that. I also got upset with Colin, because it seemed he was giving some credence to the rumours. We finally sorted it out between us, he realized I was telling the truth, and we went from barn to barn to get everything straightened out. Business actually started to pick up after that.

I had a lot of confidence in Colin. That we'd been able to go into tracks where we weren't known and do the job that we did was a great tribute to him. I had some good agents along the way, but changing agents here and there is probably not a good thing for your career. You need to find your niche. If you're not the leading rider, you need to find that someone who will make you the leading rider.

Colin Wick:
Things weren't going too good and I kind of figured out why it wasn't going too good. I would have to say it was mostly his fault, not his agent [at the time]. He was in kind of a rut, and he was getting pissed off, pulling horses up. After I'd been there a couple weeks, I said, "Don't blame your agent for all this stuff."

Gary Jones:
Wicksey was so key to Sandy because he could just get after him in a way that would motivate the heck out of him. Sandy could get down in the lip, and lot of these other agents were afraid of him when he'd get to pouting. Colin would just get after him. Sandy was just like a little kid with him. It was just a great combination, the two of them.

We did well during this time, but Colin had no plans to stay in the long term. So, I hooked up with Chick McClellan, the father of Scotty McClellan, who worked as the agent for Chris McCarron. Chick was a solid agent.

Chick McClellan:
When we got together, I explained to him that I'd be retiring in about a year or so. I'd set my life up a long time ahead to retire when I was sixty-five, and fifteen months before that he needed an agent. I'd had a heart attack in 1982 and been laid up a while, so he was my first rider after that. Sandy was a good rider, he'd won a zillion races, and was one of the nicest fellas you could ever hope to meet, a real gentleman.

* * *

In February 1983, Vicki and I decided to marry — the second time for me and the first for her. You fall in love and you're attracted to one another and you think it's going to last forever. I remember my mother asking me if I was sure I was making the right decision — because that's what mothers do. I felt I was. Chris McCarron, who broke my world record for victories only one year after I'd set it in 1973, and who had moved to the California circuit five years later, was my best man. The ceremony took place in Pasadena, in the banquet room of a place called the Castle Green. The list of invited guests included many people from the racing industry — jockeys, trainers, owners, my valet Jack Wood — and some family and friends. Not many however, from Canada.

Late in the year, I posted a significant victory with a horse called Fali Time in the Hollywood Futurity, which offered a purse of $1,049,725 — the first million-dollar race to be run in California. Fali Time was coming off a second-place finish in his previous start, the Hoist the Flag Stakes, preceded by a victory in the Norfolk Stakes — which was the first time I rode him. Co-owners Jim Mamakos and Dr. Marc Strubin liked Fali Time's chances so much that they paid the supplementary fee to enter him because the horse hadn't been kept eligible through sustaining payments. The race attracted a full field of twelve, headed by Precisionist, who had won the Hoist the Flag Stakes, and a filly, Althea, trained by D. Wayne Lukas. Precisionist went postward at just under 2–1, while Althea was second choice at just under 3–1.

Fali Time was a really neat horse to ride. He wasn't a big horse, but he just gave 110 per cent. He was trained by Gary Jones and it was exciting to ride this good horse for him.

Gary Jones:
The whole field was a Who's Who, and we came in with this little, bitty California-bred horse that was supposed to be a misfit and didn't belong and all of that. Sandy and I were on a skiing trip in Deer Valley

Lodge in Utah. I didn't want to miss the trip, but I had one important workout left with Fali Time. I had a next-door neighbor, Danny Velasquez, who was a great horseman and I asked him if he would work Fali Time and then call me and tell me how it went. Danny worked him flawlessly; meanwhile, Sandy and I were on the lifts, talking about the race and how it set up. Sandy fit the horse like a glove. We mapped the race out and it just fell into place exactly perfectly, which doesn't happen very often.

My horse was let go at more than 10–1. Precisionist set the early pace, then was overtaken by Althea after three quarters of a mile. Meanwhile, I was sitting comfortably in third and advanced to second by the top of the stretch, trailing Bold T. Jay, another longshot, who had taken the lead by a head. Then we engaged in a stretch battle in which Fali Time responded to my urging and outfinished Bold T. Jay down the lane.

Gary Jones:
Fali Time was laying just off the pace and [Bold T. Jay] went too fast and he just exploded coming into the lane. Sandy hit the horse fifty-two times in the stretch, then came back and said, "I'm sorry I had to get after him so much." He was really a lazy, little horse; kind of sore-going and lazy and didn't want to go. You literally had to make him.

Fali Time was scared to death of Sandy, and when Sandy got on him, he knew the game was on; he knew he had to run or he was going to get his little tail whipped.

We were so excited because we had a [Kentucky] Derby horse. We'd just gotten back from a fun trip and it was just kind of a dream week — the whole deal.

What a thrill to win the first million-dollar race in California! I remember John Tyre, a Californian who had put himself through law school by working in the parking lots at the racetracks and who would become one of my best friends, actually asked for my autograph after I won with Fali Time. I was so happy that I was shaking as I signed his program.

John Tyre:
They had a special race program that day, and as Sandy walked by I said, "Hey, you want to autograph right here where it says Fali Time?" He couldn't even write — his hand was shaking so bad. After winning a million-dollar race, you're so geared up, and he was shaking because he was so excited. That was a pretty big race at the time.

I finished the season with purse earnings of just under $4 million, which placed me thirteenth overall on the continent. I had only 136 wins from 1,089 mounts, but I had high hopes that Fali Time could be my ticket to the Derby the following May. Fali Time won the California Breeders Champion Stakes early in January. Things were going well for both me and the horse, but then we both encountered some problems. Later in the month, I suffered a fractured vertebrae below my rib cage when the filly I was riding stumbled leaving the gate. I was third in the jockey standings at Santa Anita at the time of the injury.

It's hard to be injured when there are so many jockeys lining up to get your mounts. I was only expected to be out a few weeks, but I missed some mounts on Fali Time because of the injury. He lost a couple of times before bouncing back and winning the San Felipe Stakes in late March by a neck as the 3–2 favourite. Next came the Santa Anita Derby, the major stepping stone in California en route to the Kentucky Derby. The favourite in the race was Precisionist, who had won the San Rafael Stakes in his last start and was bet down to 11–10 in the Santa Anita Derby. My horse was the second choice at just under 3–1. Precisionist charged out to an early lead under Chris McCarron and I was tracking him in second, but Precisionist had too much in reserve and led by three lengths at the top of the stretch, running at a very fast clip. He gave way, with a sixteenth of a mile to go, to 32–1 outsider Mighty Adversary and lost by a length and a half in a time of 1:49 for the mile and an eighth. I finished fourth by almost four lengths.

We felt Fali Time might like a little bit of a softer racetrack, so we decided to go on to the Derby. A total of twenty horses were entered in the race, including two fillies trained by D. Wayne Lukas, Althea and Life's Magic, who were coupled as an entry and went postward as the favourite at just under 3–1. Althea had beaten ten male horses in the Arkansas Derby, winning the mile-and-one-eighth race by seven lengths in track-record time. Only a week earlier, she had run against a field of fillies in the Fantasy Stakes, finishing second by three-quarters of a length at 3–5 odds. Life's Magic came into the Derby winless in three starts on the season, including running third to Althea in a stakes race.

Second choice in the wagering, at about 7–2, was Swale, the Florida Derby winner who had been upset at 1–10 odds in the Lexington Stakes. I had Fali Time racing comfortably in seventh, about three and a half lengths behind the leader, after three quarters of a mile. Then I made my move. At the head of the stretch, however, Swale had drawn off to lead by five lengths and finished first by three and a half. I placed fifth by six lengths.

I claimed foul against Gate Dancer's rider, Eddie Delahoussaye, for repeated bumping in the stretch. The stewards also lodged an inquiry. Gate Dancer was demoted from fourth to fifth, while Fali Time moved up one place. Gate Dancer was the type of horse that used to wear the big earmuffs. He was a bit of a rogue, and sometimes he would duck in, sometimes he would duck out. Eddie and I were both making our moves at the same time. Gate Dancer ducked in and bumped me on the heels of the horse in front of me, and I actually had to stand up and grab Fali Time and check him before I started riding him again. It really took a lot of momentum from him. Had it not been for the bumping, I think I would have finished a lot closer than fifth — I think I could have made second or third.

Gary Jones:
I went down to trackside to claim foul — I couldn't get down because there were so many people — and Sandy had already claimed it. We were flabbergasted when they changed it. It didn't do us much good — they changed us from fifth to fourth — but at least we got a cheque in the Derby.

Historically, the Derby is no holds barred; whoever gets to the finish line first, that's the way it happens. It's too prestigious of a race for the stewards to be changing the order of finish on an inquiry. Everybody knew it. That's the way the game was played back then when you were running in the Derby.

We would have been third probably or second; we weren't going to beat Swale.

* * *

It was around this time that I started working with an agent named John DeSantis, who was friends with Chris McCarron. And because I was good friends with Chris, John and I became acquainted. He grew up in Philadelphia and moved to California in the mid-'70s to go to college, around the time I started to do really well.

John DeSantis:
The first time I met Sandy, he was so nice and such a great person that I said to myself, "Man, this guy has a great line of BS. He has really got it down."

The second time I met him, the same reaction. I thought to myself, "This guy doesn't let up." We'd golf together and I'd think, "This guy, he's really got a good game going on here."

But as time went on, I got to know him better and I realized that it wasn't phony. That was Sandy. He's just one of the nicest people you would ever meet in your entire life — generous, caring — just a nice person.

And he was so competitive, and I think this part of it was what made him so great. You always hear about great athletes who are fiercely competitive. Whether he was playing golf or a table-hockey game or tennis, it didn't matter: he wanted to win.

That transferred over to the riding part of it. He was not a great student of the game, not along the lines of Jerry Bailey or Chris McCarron. He was more in the Pincay mould. He just rode horses and he wanted to win so badly, and he transferred that to the horse. He wasn't a guy who was going to sit down and study films or tapes or which owners to schmooze or the right thing to say. He never had to worry about what he said because he was such a nice person. He just said nice things naturally. But he wasn't a really student of the game. He wasn't a strategist. He was just a plain, hard, competitor; a tough competitor.

When I took over as Sandy's agent, there was kind of a surge. It was kind of a rejuvenation. It's like getting a new coach for a football team. We did well for a while in California, and then it kind of settled down again.

Gary Jones:
Business just fell off a little bit. New guys came around — Gary Stevens got going — and there were too many short fields. At the time, I was a pretty big outfit and I wasn't using him as much. He just kind of got into that pouty stage, as he would every once in a while, and Wicksey wasn't there to boost him up, so it just kind of fell apart on him.

I don't think Sandy ever forgave me for it. I still think the world of him, regardless of how he feels about me. I saw him at the Breeders' Cup in 2004 at it was like old home week. I hadn't seen him in so long and it was really good to see him.

I kind of felt bad about what happened to him because I know I had a lot to do with maybe being part of the reason he went back to Canada [in 1988]. It wasn't because he was any different of a rider. A great rider is a great rider — it doesn't make any difference, they don't lose their ability. They're like a great trainer; they're only as good as the horse they're on.

It was just one of those things — and I always felt Sandy held it against me and I always felt bad about it — but business is business. It happened with Chris McCarron and I, and we're still best of friends. Those things happen. You go along and you're in the heat of battle and whoever is doing good, you kind of want to lean that way.

It makes it easier on a trainer because they don't have to cool their owners out. "What do you have Hawley on there for? We could have had Stevens. How come McCarron's not on this horse? Don't you have any pull with these guys?" That kind of deal. It's a stress that a lot of trainers will fall to, and it's unfortunate, but that's part of the stress that goes with the business. It's just the owner putting pressure on you and you falling into the trap instead of just saying, "I'm going to stick with this guy."

It never had anything to do with Sandy's riding. Ever. It's just the way it was at the time. It's the flavour of the month.

I found in California that they do like new faces. The same thing had happened when I'd first gone there — I'd started riding horses that other guys were riding, when *I* was the new face. When Gary Stevens first came there, he didn't really do well, but when he caught on, people were saying things like, "Oh, he's a hot rider." Gary Jones might have wanted to continue to ride me, but as a trainer you'll get into a battle against the owners to keep the rider you want versus what they want. And, of course, the owners are going to win because they pay the bills.

I always liked Gary and I never took it personally anytime I was taken off a horse. Of course I felt badly about it, but never took it personally. It's like Gary said when I saw him at the Breeders' Cup in 2004: there were no hard feelings. You try and remember the good things. You don't think about the bad things, because there were times when I had to take off a trainer's or owners' horse and ride someone else's instead. They don't really hold it against you. Of course they wish they still had you riding for them, but they don't really hold a grudge.

I finished the year with 169 wins from 1,127 mounts and purse earnings of $4,239,808, which placed me fourteenth in the continent.

The fall of 1984 was marked by a major event in the racing industry with the inaugural running of the Breeders' Cup, which came to be billed as the Super Bowl of thoroughbred racing. The first-ever event took place November 10 at Hollywood Park, and it brought together horses from around the world for seven separate races totalling $10 million in purses. Championships could be won and lost based on performances in the races, which were televised live.

The opening race was the $1 million Juvenile for two-year-old colts and geldings, followed by the $1 million Juvenile Fillies, the $1 million Sprint for horses of any age or sex, the $1 million Mile on the grass, the $1 million Distaff for fillies and mares, the $2 million Turf for long-distance grass horses and the $3 million Classic for horse of any age or sex running the classic dirt distance of a mile and a quarter.

It was a big deal, and part of the excitement revolved around wondering whether the idea of the Breeders' Cup was going to catch on. I was pleased to have a few mounts in the inaugural event: Tonzarun in the Mile, Comedy Act in the Distaff and Treizieme in the Turf. They were all longshots, unfortunately: Tonzarun was a 45–1 shot who ran sixth by some three lengths in the Mile; Comedy Act went out at 44–1 and ran fourth by nine and a half lengths in the Distaff; and Treizieme, who was my best hope at just under 15–1, ran last in the Turf after showing some early speed.

It would have been great to have a couple of favourites to ride. I think the Breeders' Cup just came too late in my career. Had it been launched earlier in my career, when my business was a lot better, it probably would have been better for me personally. But I think it was great for the sport overall. I used to enjoy it even when I didn't have a mount, and even today it's one of my favourite days of the year.

CHAPTER EIGHT

Fighting Cancer

As 1985 ended, it was becoming obvious that I had reached a critical point in my career in California. My business wasn't as strong as it had been, so I made the decision to leave in April for a four-month stint at Canterbury Downs in Minnesota. It proved to be one of the most significant moves of my career. Canterbury was about to begin its second season and had been looking for a top rider. The track's general manager, Nat Wess, who was the former media director at Hollywood Park, said it would be great for publicity if I gave Minnesota a shot. He mentioned that a lot of trainers there would be interested in giving me mounts and felt it would be very good for my career as well.

Nat Wess:
We were looking for name riders, but by the same token, Sandy's career at that time wasn't going anywhere. It appeared this was going to be a good spot for him, where he could come in and ride the full card every day. With the riders that we had, I was pretty confident he would be the leading rider. I thought he was head and shoulders above everything we had there.

Among the trainers at Canterbury was Carl Nafzger, who would go on to win the Kentucky Derby and the Breeders' Cup Classic in 1990 with Unbridled, the eventual horse of the year in North America. My agent, John DeSantis, and I just thought we'd go there and see how we liked it.

John DeSantis:
Business in California had stalled, and it seemed like a good idea at the time. It was kind of like a chicken-

and-egg question: are you not winning because you're not riding good horses, or are you not riding good horses because you're not winning? It kind of goes in circles. When your main client doesn't continue to support you, you're not going to win as much, and then other people aren't going to support you because you're not winning.

Certainly, Nat was influential in persuading Sandy and me to go there. I'd been with Sandy about three or four years at the time. We had become very good friends besides agent and jockey. I went ahead to Minnesota without him a couple weeks in advance of the meeting, just to kind of survey the situation, meet some of the trainers and kind of build a foundation. It was freezing cold, and I was walking through this barn area when I came upon a stall with a guy inside, working the pitchfork and laying in the straw bedding.

I said to him, "Hi, I'm Johnny D. I'm a jock's agent."

He said, "Yeah, who do you got?"

I said, "I got Sandy Hawley."

"Oh, yeah?" he said. "Where's she been riding?"

Here's this future Hall of Fame jockey who's going to Minnesota, and that's one of the receptions we got. At that moment, I thought, "Oh, God, what have we done?"

I remember asking Vicki to come to Minnesota with me, and I remember her saying she didn't like Minnesota. Even though she hadn't spent any time there, she didn't like the idea of it and didn't want to go, although she did come for a brief visit during the three months I was away. I could see at that time that the marriage was falling apart. She had been taking acting lessons for a few years and wasn't about to follow me around. I could see the writing on the wall.

I returned to Woodbine on June 22 to receive the Avelino Gomez Memorial Award for contributions to racing in Canada. I can't tell you how special it was to accept an award named after one of my idols. I was only four wins away from the 5,000 mark at the time, and I considered accomplishing the feat at home, but Minnesota had been good to me and I wanted to give something back to the fans. Things were going very well, and the people at Canterbury were treating us very well. They were going to pull out the stops to publicize my 5,000th win. It would be a real benefit for Canterbury Downs for me to do it there, too.

While I was at Woodbine, Bruce Walker asked if he could have the whip from my 5,000th win, and I agreed to give it to him. I notched number 5,000 on June 26, 1986, aboard a horse called Mighty Massa, who was trained by Kathy Walsh and owned by Carol and John Roy. True to my word, I saved the whip for Bruce; I also gave the boots I wore in that race to my former valet, Ronnie Robinson, because he was like a father to me. (In a gesture that epitomizes how classy he is, he gave the boots back to Lisa and me in later years as a keepsake for our children.) I probably should have kept souvenirs of my important races, but if good friends asked for them, I didn't mind giving them away.

While riding in Minnesota, I decided to go to a tanning booth. I'd heard about them, and thought I'd give it a shot. Shortly afterward, I asked John DeSantis to take a look at something on my back that my silks were rubbing against and that was bothering me. He took a look and said it didn't look like anything special, just a mole. I couldn't see anything in the mirror. I decided to have it examined by Dr. Dan Capen, a top orthopedic surgeon and a horse owner, when I returned to California.

We actually didn't ride the entire meet in Minnesota; instead, we went to Chicago to ride a bunch of horses for Carl Nafzger, who'd sent part of his stable to Arlington Park. It was a great experience in so many ways. I became good friends with jockey Gerry Gallitano, who had a beautiful house on a golf course — which suited me fine; I loved golf. And the fans were a pleasant surprise. When I got beat on an even-money shot, my first thought was, "Uh-oh, here I am in Chicago, a big, tough city. They'll probably give me the same treatment I got in New York." Some of the New York fans would get pretty obnoxious when I'd get beat on a favourite. But the Chicago fans couldn't have been more different. A couple of people said, "Good try," while another said, "Good luck next time." I thought the fans were different than anywhere else because they were so forgiving. I ended up tying Pat Day for the leading-rider title, and then John DeSantis and I returned to Minnesota, where we clinched the riding title at Canterbury by two wins over Mike Smith, who had won the title in the track's inaugural year.

John DeSantis:
That Minnesota meet was a very strong meet for trainers. There was an incredible assortment of people at that racetrack. And the Minnesota experience was very good for Sandy. He won a lot of races, and the top trainers — Billy Mott, Carl Nafzger, Jerry Calvin and those kind — were using him.

When we got to Arlington, trainer Jack Van Berg was having breakfast by the track one morning and I came by and sat down with him. He was asking me about riding some horses for him, and then he said, "How'd you get this jock back riding so fast?"

The whole Minnesota experience rejuvenated Sandy's confidence in himself and confidence in his abilities. I don't think his abilities had ever waned. It's just that California is very fashionable. They go for the hot rider, and there were some new guys. But that time in Minnesota, Chicago and later in Kentucky all reinvigorated his confidence. He was riding great at that time.

* * *

When I returned to California about a month later, I went to see Dr. Capen. He didn't like the look of the mole, and sent me to a plastic surgeon to have it removed and sent for analysis. I probably should have had it looked at right away. The surgery left a one-inch scar. I was told that I could continue riding because it would take a week or so for the results to come back; in the meantime, I went to Kentucky to ride in a stakes race. I was in the shower after the race, and there was only one other jockey there — I don't remember who it was — and he asked about my scar. I told him I'd just gotten a mole removed, but that the plastic surgeon advised me not to worry about it — just to stay out of the sun. The jockey asked, "It wasn't malignant melanoma, was it?"

At the time I didn't know what that was, so I repeated, "No, no. He just told me to stay out of the sun."

"Well, that's a good thing," the jockey replied. "I had a buddy of mine who had it, and he only lasted for two months."

The plastic surgeon called me after my return from Kentucky and told me to come in right away because he had the results of my biopsy. I went in, and he told me he had bad news: the mole on my back was malignant melanoma, and it had already reached the fifth level, deep into the skin.

Melanoma originates in the melanocytes, the cells near the top layer of skin that contain pigment. When it spreads, it moves downwards into the skin, and from there can then spread further — to the lymph nodes, lungs, liver, brain or bones. There are five levels of penetration, the deepest or worst being the fifth level, which is the fat layer under the skin. There are also four stages of the cancer; at stages one and two, the cancer is found in the skin; at stage three it has reached the lymph nodes; and stage four is widespread disease. I had stage two, which was later reclassified to stage three when a tumorous lymph node was discovered during surgery, and then, after a second operation months later, stage four.

After leaving the doctor's office I was driving home and remembering what the jockey had said in Kentucky. And what pops into my head? "I'll never find out who wins the Stanley Cup this year!" It's crazy what you think about when you think you're going to die.

Vicki and I started searching for a cancer specialist, and we got in touch with Dr. James Helsper in Pasadena. When I visited him, he said, "We're going to have to operate right away. The biopsy doesn't look good. We're going to have to do some major surgery." Being from the track, I naturally asked him what my odds were. "Every patient is different," he replied, then tried to talk around it a little bit. All I could think was that

I was a goner. I pray every day, but when you find out you have a serious illness, you pray a whole lot more. That's what I did.

Reports at the time indicated that melanoma had been on the rise in southern California and other year-round warm-weather climates because of frequent exposure to harmful ultraviolet rays from sunlight. The American Cancer Institute reported that of the 450,000 cases of skin cancer diagnosed every year in America, 22,000 people develop malignant melanoma and about 5,500 die from it.

The Breeders' Cup was only a couple weeks away, and I had a couple of mounts for Carl Nafzger: Zero Minus in the Juvenile Fillies and Orono in the Juvenile. Dr. Helsper said I needed the operation, but that I could wait a week or two to have it. Both of my horses were coming off wins but were rated as longshots in the morning line, went postward at high odds and finished far back in their respective races.

Jim Bannon, who did the morning line and handicapping for the Ontario Jockey Club, was conducting a handicapping seminar at the Breeders' Cup and he brought a large group with him. It was really nice to see so many Canadians. I remember talking to Jim about the surgery and telling him it wasn't looking great, but that I had a great surgeon. A few days later I had the operation.

Jim Bannon:
I remember feeling so unnerved about it that I cried all the way home to Toronto on the plane. It was so strange because we had not known Sandy for anything but his strength at that time, and for him to be suddenly vulnerable was quite different than I had ever known him.

Prior to going under the knife, Dr. Helsper told me, "I won't lie to you: it really doesn't look good. When I do this surgery, I'm going to have to go in there and see what I find. I may have to cut muscle in the back. I'll do the best I can, but if I keep finding cancer, I'm going to have to keep cutting. You're going to have to sign a waiver release because I might have to cut so much muscle that it could end your career. You won't be able to lift your arms."

At that point I was focused completely on saving my life, so I signed the paper and told him, "Just do what you have to do to save my life. If worse comes to worst, I'll have to find something else to do." Vicki and I were a little bit on the outs, but it wasn't to the point where we were going to get a divorce. She was there for me one hundred per cent, including coming to the hospital the day I had my surgery. John DeSantis was also there when Dr. Helsper performed the operation. In my mind, John was like a young Colin Wick — a great agent and quite a character. We had been in Minnesota and all over the place together, and now he was there for me, offering all his support.

John DeSantis:
The doctor told Vicki and me that Sandy was not supposed to live. I don't remember if it was a year or six months or eighteen months. I don't remember an exact number. I remember a year. Maybe the doctor gave a couple numbers, but Sandy was not supposed to live. The doctor made that pretty clear that he was not expecting him to live.

That was devastating. Not only was representing Sandy my job, but he was my friend. On racing days we were together. We golfed together. We watched sports together. We played tennis. Table games. We competed against each other. We were more like brothers than jockey and agent, and to hear that news was devastating.

It wasn't delivered in a maybe way. The doctor just laid it out because they found it in his lymph nodes, and at that time that was a death sentence.

A lot of people from Minnesota sent me these huge get-well cards, which was very touching. John stayed overnight, sleeping in a chair, and was there when I woke up after the surgery. I asked him how long the surgery had taken, and he told me it had been five hours and that it seemed to have gone well. Dr. Helsper came in shortly after that and confirmed it had been five hours and that he had taken a large area off my back, where the mole had initially been, and removed thirty-two lymph glands from under my arm to see if it had spread. He found one microscopic trace that showed it had spread. He said it was better to have just a microscopic trace of it in the lymph glands than to have it right through all the lymph glands: it meant there was a chance that it might not spread. He was a wonderful surgeon, and did a great job. I really don't have too bad of a scar on my back, especially when I consider the surgery that had to be done.

I couldn't ride, so I went home to Canada for Christmas, to spend time with my parents. Vicki accompanied me. It was a very emotional time — I was convinced it was nearly the end for me. Even though the doctor tells you it looks pretty good, you've still got doubts in the back of your mind. Just the idea of being operated on for melanoma is scary enough. I talked to a lot of friends who were doctors, as well as others who were familiar with malignant melanoma. I tried to find out whatever I could from anybody that knew anything about medicine, trying to get feedback. It was always the same scenario, "Every patient is different."

Des Hawley:
It was quite a traumatic time. He enjoyed his stay while he was here, and when he felt the urge to go back, he went back. It was a good thing that he did come home. We were quite concerned about him. As he progressed, he started feeling better. He got good vibes from his doctor, and that was quite helpful. With the reports that we were getting from his doctor and the people we knew down there, and from his own feelings about it, we were quite assured that he would battle it out and get over it.

Tom Slater, who covered horse racing for the *Toronto Star*, came to California to do a story about me. It ran under the headline "Hawley Doing Well after Cancer Surgery," and in addition to detailing the surgery and how I was adjusting to my recovery, it summed up my career. Tom won a Sovereign Award the following year for best newspaper story, and while I wasn't there, I'm told that he gave a very emotional acceptance speech in which he essentially said he hoped he wouldn't have to write a follow-up story about my health for a long time.

It took me more than two months to physically recover from the operation. I had a lot of swelling underneath my arm where the lymph glands had been removed. And I had to go and get my arm drained every week. Dr. Helsper would use a long syringe to drain the area under my arm and take a look to see how everything was coming along. I was told that swimming was the best form of exercise for my rehab. Fortunately, my good friend Don Pierce, one of the top riders in California at the time, had a house with a swimming pool that he heated just for me so that I could swim. It was wonderful. Don had a sense of humour, too. Once, when I told him that I still felt a little cold in the pool, he said: "Get your butt in there. I heated it just for you." That's the way I got back in shape. I started galloping horses again in late January in preparation for my return to Santa Anita.

John DeSantis:
Through all the terror over his sickness, he never once believed that it wasn't going to be okay. Outwardly, he never let on that he was as sick as the doctors said he was. He always kept a positive attitude about things, always looking ahead, always saying, "Where are we going to go this year?" Here's a guy who won more than 5,000 races and then was faced with cancer and death, and he refused to give up.

* * *

My return came on February 1, exactly three months after the Breeders' Cup. The guys in the jocks' room were behind me one hundred percent — even guys I'd had run-ins with. I mean, we all pretty much get along, but every so often you might have a bit of a thing with some of the riders. For instance, Martin Pedroza was a bit of an enemy of mine, because we'd had a few run-ins on the track, shutting each other off, but even he was good to me on my return. All the riders were very supportive throughout the whole ordeal.

I'll never forget that first race. It was as if I was riding in the first race of my career. I rode a horse called Rodney, and I was leading all the way. Coming down the stretch, I thought I had it won. In the last seventy yards my horse was getting tired — and so was I — and Laffit Pincay came up behind me and won in the final stride. I rode in three other races, but didn't finish in the top three in any of them.

I decided to return to Arkansas, because that's where trainers like Carl Nafzger, for whom I'd done well before, were going to be. We had a lot of mounts, and it looked like things were going to be fine, but only two weeks into my return I suffered an injury. A horse in front of me snapped a leg and fell down, and I tumbled in the ensuing collision. I was treated for a sore back — I remember having to crawl into bed on my hands and knees. More than anything, it was very frustrating. Here I was, just trying to get going again, and I had to overcome another setback. Still, John and I went to Keeneland in Kentucky for the spring meet, and things improved.

John DeSantis:
We were at Hot Springs, and we told everyone we were going to Keeneland. A girl exercise rider told me, "You have to go see trainer Neil Howard. He wins all the races at Keeneland."

I got to Keeneland and went to Neil Howard's tack room and said, "I've got Sandy Hawley's book. Do you have any place you can use us?" He looked at one of his exercise riders, who was sitting on one of the tack boxes, and kind of grunted at her, then motioned with his head, and she left.

"Sit down," he said.

So I went in and he proceeded to flip through the condition book, marking all kinds of races. I said, "Are these all calls for Sandy to ride?"

"Yeah," he said. "Why? What do people usually do when you say you have Sandy Hawley?"

We had success at the Keeneland spring meet, where we led with nineteen wins, including three stakes. Then it was off to Chicago for Arlington's meet. In June, I had another cancer scare — I found these bumps on my neck. I went to John and said, "It doesn't look good — they're getting a little bit bigger." We decided to go back to California after the meet ended, and I went to see Dr. Helsper again.

"With your history," he said, "we're going to have to do another operation." Before the operation, I had to sign another waiver. The doctor told me that if, during the course of the surgery, he found that the cancer had spread beyond my neck, he might need to remove a portion of my neck — either through a procedure called a modified neck dissection, which removes a portion of it, or possibly a radical dissection, which removes half of your neck.

I told him to do what he had to in order to save me. As I went under the anaesthetic, I thought, "Geez, I might end up coming out of the operation with half a neck." When I woke up, John DeSantis was there again. He told me the surgery had taken three hours and that they hadn't had to remove any of my neck. That was a great relief. Dr. Helsper thought he'd got all of the melanoma this time. He'd taken some lymph glands from the side of my neck and found no trace of cancer.

After that, I was referred to Dr. Malcolm Mitchell, an oncologist who is head of immunotherapy at the University of Southern California's Norris Cancer Center. He put me on an experimental therapeutic vaccine — called a theraccine for short. Years later, in a story about me published in the March 1993 Norris Cancer Center report, Dr. Mitchell explained that the term theraccine was coined to distinguish it from the usual vaccines because it treated existing cancer cells rather than preventing cancer the way vaccines prevent viral illnesses. He also explained that this particular theraccine stimulates the immune system, not only to shrink measurable tumours but, more importantly, to halt the spread (or metastasis) of the disease, thus prolonging a person's life. The theraccine was developed from melanoma cells obtained from biopsies from two different patients. The cells were chopped up in a sterile blender, then mixed with an immunological booster substance. It was injected under the skin of the buttocks and arms — but not into the tumour itself — first weekly and eventually monthly to maintain responses.

The program consisted of a series of five shots administered over six weeks. The drug was relatively new, and it was unclear as to how safe it was. I remember being hopeful that it might save my life. In the article about me, Dr. Mitchell said he couldn't be absolutely certain how long I might have been expected to live; based on all the research he was aware of, the average time of survival from the first time the disease appeared is between six and twelve months.

Much has changed since then. In those days, only late-stage melanoma patients were being treated with the theraccine. Now it is being used to treat people who have had their primary melanoma removed.

When I was told about the vaccine, it reminded me of something that had happened at the beginning of my riding career. I'd had warts on my hands that kept getting worse and worse. When I'd ride at Greenwood in the fall, the cold would make them crack and bleed. You'd barely see parts of my hands under all the Band-Aids and such that I'd put on my fingers for protection. I tried to have the warts burnt off, cut off, frozen off, yet they'd keep coming back, worse than ever. A vaccine ended up being the cure. George Gardiner, an owner for whom I rode quite often, told me he had a doctor who made up a vaccine from warts. I went to this doctor, who took a portion of the wart and blended it into a vaccine. Within about six months of taking the shots, the warts were gone. So, when Dr. Mitchell told me he was going to take some of my melanoma cells to make a vaccine, that really gave me confidence. I think that it's very important to be optimistic that something's going to work. A lot of the time it's mind over matter.

I started taking the vaccine pretty soon after I had the second operation, when I had only small lumps under my skin, and I believe it saved my life. Dr. Mitchell is not only a genius, but also a very personable and nice guy. He took his time with me and he gave me reason to hope, which I really believed helped me as well.

I should point out that by this time, Vicki and I had separated. I moved in with John Tyre, and he saw firsthand the physical results of the shots. I have little dents in the back of my arms and hip where I used to get the shots, where they produced swelling.

John Tyre:
He used to come home after the shots, and the first day after a shot he'd feel fine, but the next day he'd be just miserable physically because it hurt. But he always believed that what he was going through was going to make him better.

* * *

In July, shortly after I was given clearance to resume riding, I returned to Woodbine to ride a horse called Bold Executive in the Plate Trial Stakes. The colt finished second by two and a half lengths to Afleet, a horse many people considered to be the best in Canada at that time. Despite the second-place finish, Bold Executive's owners were encouraged to run the colt two weeks later in the Plate and they asked me to ride him. It was a great feeling to come back home. Not only did I get a chance to come back and ride, but it was also great to be with my parents again. Amidst all the turmoil, being back in Canada really felt like being at home again. My horse, who was really stretching his capabilities to run a mile and a quarter, finished eighth in the Plate, almost fifteen lengths behind upset winner Market Control, who led Afleet by three and a half lengths. The third-place finisher was Afleet's stablemate, One from Heaven, who was ridden by Bill Shoemaker. I wish my horse had run a bit better in the Plate, but he had a great race against a very strong horse in Afleet.

I returned to California, but came back in October to ride Highland Ruckus, a full brother to Bold Executive, in the Grey Stakes. If the colt did well, he would be pointed towards the

Breeders' Cup Juvenile, but he finished sixth in the twelve-horse field. I had one mount in the Breeders' — Pearlie Gold in the Juvenile Fillies. On the eve of the Cup, I had just finished welcoming a group of visiting Canadians at a seminar hosted by racing analyst Jim Bannon in the Century City Hotel. Jim and I took the elevator down to the bottom level and when the doors opened, Bob Hope was standing there waiting to go in and go up. Jim was so excited seeing the famous comedian, he blurted out, "Bob Hope." Without missing a beat, Hope exclaimed, "Sandy Hawley." He and I had a big laugh together and a great chat.

Pearlie Gold wasn't given much of a shot by the bettors, who made her the longest shot in the field of twelve at odds of more than 71–1, but she didn't run too badly, finishing fifth by only about three and a half lengths.

We finished the season with 151 wins from only 837 mounts, but earned purses just shy of $3 million. Some people thought I should have won the award for the Comeback Rider of the Year, but the voters chose Chris McCarron, who recovered from a broken leg the year before to win the Kentucky Derby and the Breeders' Cup Classic with the eventual horse of the year, Alysheba.

During my returns to Woodbine, my former agent, Colin Wick, suggested that if I came back to ride full time in Canada there would be a lot of trainers and owners interested in my services. "Why don't you think about it?" he asked.

I began to give it serious consideration. I'd just been through a scary time, and I hadn't been spending much time with my parents — maybe a month out of the year, if that. I decided during the new year to take up Colin on his offer and return to Canada to ride full time for the first time in ten years.

I told Vicki about my plans and that I'd like her to come with me. I was giving her the choice, though I had a feeling she would to say no anyway. I had my mind made up, however: I was coming back to Canada no matter what. I felt it would be good for me emotionally. She said she'd prefer to stay in California — she was taking acting lessons and, she said, "I'm a California girl."

She said, "You go to Canada and ride your races and come and visit me. We can stay married, and you can come down to California in the winters." But I knew it wouldn't work that way; I was headed for my second divorce. In time, Vicki remarried, and so did I. We've both gotten on with our lives and haven't had any contact with one another for several years.

CHAPTER NINE

Home Again

After an absence of almost ten years, I finally decided to return to Canada. I had just recorded 23 wins from my first 201 mounts in 1988 and was in the top five in wins at the Santa Anita meet. In past years, I would have headed back north in June, in time for the big Canadian races, but this year I figured it would be better to be at Woodbine for the start of the six-month meet in late April. The purses had grown substantially and were now just below California and New York, but beyond the money I felt it I had a chance to get off to a strong start and rebuild connections, through Colin Wick, with the top barns.

I arrived a couple days before the start of the meet and took part in numerous interviews set up by Bruce Walker, the Ontario Jockey Club's publicity director. As I walked around the Woodbine backstretch, I was greeted by many old friends. The weather was crisp on the first day of the meet, and Colin had lined up several mounts for me. My first two had the lead going into the stretch, but couldn't hold it to the wire. It always seems that the first win is the toughest to get — and once you get that first one, you're on your way. I did it with my third mount, King Condo, in the fifth race, and the crowd of 16,657 gave me a hearty cheer. King Condo's owner was Marty Atkins, who was known as the king of condominiums in the Toronto area at the time. I remember him very well because we became good friends. He later gave me a book on macrobiotics, a way of eating designed to free the body of toxins by eliminating foods containing processed sugars, salts, red meat, red fish and certain vegetables. Instead, you eat foods that pass through the system in a matter of hours. I believed it was the thing to do to promote my health and beat the cancer. I watch my diet even today because of that book.

We started getting a lot of mounts from Sam-Son Farm, one of the top outfits at the time, and won the Canadian Oaks — for the seventh time in my career — with Tilt My Halo. She was the 7–20 favourite and won by three-quarters of a length. She ran a little bit green through the stretch, but she was a nice horse and at the end of the season was named the champion three-year-old filly in Canada.

The Queen's Plate was three weeks later, and I had a solid mount in Regal Classic, who had run in the Kentucky Derby, placing fifth, and then in the Preakness Stakes, placing sixth. He came home for the Canadian Triple Crown, and en route he won the Marine Stakes and the Plate Trial Stakes. I picked up the mount for his Canadian campaign. Owner/breeder Ernie Samuel and trainer Jim Day also entered Regal Intention in the Plate. He had run exclusively in Canada and had developed into a solid stablemate, winning several stakes races, including the Victoria Park a week before the Plate. But the main focus was on Regal Classic, who had come from a champion family out of one of Mr. Samuel's top broodmares, No Class, and sired by Vice Regent, one of the top stallions in Canada. Regal Intention was also well bred, by Vice Regent out of Tiffany Tam, another of Mr. Samuel's quality broodmares. The two horses went postward as the favourites in the field of eleven at slightly more than 1–2. Jack Lauzon rode Regal Intention, who sat behind the pacesetter for almost a mile, then took over the lead and won by three and a half lengths. Regal Classic just didn't have enough to catch him through the stretch. It was disappointing, because I had missed my chance to win a record fifth Plate. But it was Jack's first win, on his twelfth try.

Two weeks later, we hooked up again in the Prince Of Wales Stakes at Fort Erie, although the real drama happened before the race. Jack Lauzon and a couple of other jockeys, who rode at Woodbine earlier in the day, set out for Fort Erie in a helicopter that was forced down by a lightning storm about 35 miles (or 50 kilometres) from the track. Jack went to an individual's home and called the stewards, notifying them of what had happened and the possibility that they might miss the race. The pilot was able to start the helicopter again, and Jack and the other jockeys arrived about six minutes or so before post time. I had driven to Fort Erie the night before. Jack and I engaged in a thrilling duel in which I placed my horse closer to Regal Intention, who led from the outset. Heading into the stretch, Regal Intention led by a head, but I just got up in the final stride to win by a nose. The race was run on a sloppy track, and I don't think my horse liked the footing.

Both horses were kept out of the Breeders' Stakes because Sam-Son had great depth and opted to run the entry of King's Deputy and Hang the Expense. I had the mount on King's Deputy, who won by a head. That meant Sam-Son won all three legs of the Canadian Triple Crown — with three different horses!

Regal Classic ran in the Arlington Million, which had been shifted to Woodbine while Chicago's Arlington Park underwent some renovations. Regal Classic faced older, seasoned grass horses, some of whom had been shipped in from Europe because the Arlington Million was, naturally, a million-dollar race. It was a tough assignment, and he finished last in the field of fourteen, leading for half a mile but tiring in the final mile. After that, he was pointed to the inaugural Molson Export Million, another million-dollar race, this one for three-year-olds on the dirt. It drew a field of seven and he ran second by half a length. He always gave one hundred per cent.

Overall, it turned out to be a great year. We won 19 stakes races and led the Woodbine meet with a record 190 winners from 751 mounts and purse earnings of more than $4.1 million. I had 196 winners in Canada and set a national record for purse earnings with more than $4.4 million.

At the end of the year, I won the Sovereign Award for top jockey and received a special Sovereign Award as Man of the Year. The latter award was especially surprising — hard to believe, in fact. They don't hand out a Man of the Year Award every year, and they don't notify the winner in advance — I didn't have a speech prepared for that part, but it was just a tremendous honour.

I returned to ride in California in the latter part of 1988 and lived with John Tyre. I even had John eating a macrobiotic diet. He didn't mind trying it, because he figured it was healthy for him, too. Our favourite dinner meal consisted of a wheat-flour pizza with broccoli, mushrooms, onions and a ton of soy cheese. John was there while I was going through my vaccine therapy.

Early in the new year, at Santa Anita, I suffered a painful accident when my mount stumbled crossing the finish line and stepped on me as it got up. It was an unusually muddy day and the races were run over a deep, heavy track. And my horse hadn't run for a year. I actually stood up at the wire, and the horse didn't even take a bad step — he just went straight down. Luckily, the messy track made for a soft landing. When I hit the ground I thought, "Oh, good, I'm okay." Then, when the horse got up, he actually ran right over top of me and stepped on my ribs, cracking four of them. It took a while to heal, and it was a very uncomfortable ordeal. The reason it took a bit longer than expected to heal was that, when I sneezed, I'd reaggravate the injury. It basically kept me off my mounts for a month.

Shortly thereafter, I went to ride in New Orleans, which had its annual meet at the Fair Grounds. I was scheduled to ride a lot of horses for Jim Day, the trainer for Sam-Son Farm, but I was involved in a terrible spill on my first day there. The second horse I rode went down, and I hit the ground face first. I didn't break any bones, but it was one of the hardest spills I'd had to that point in my career. I ended up with a concussion; the funny thing is, again, the horse didn't take a bad step, but just went down abruptly. When she fell with me, it was on the turf; I was in the lead, we were coming down the stretch and all of a sudden, at the seventy-yard pole, she just seemed to tilt over to the left.

When they loaded me into the ambulance, there was a girl paramedic. "Where am I?" I asked her. "What racetrack am I at?" She said, "You're at the Fair Grounds in New Orleans." The last thing I could remember was being in California. They took me back to the infirmary, and I was accompanied in the ambulance by my dad. He'd come with me to California and had driven with me to New Orleans. He was also planning to go to Kentucky, where I had intended to ride after New

Orleans. I remember seeing him in the ambulance and thinking, "What the heck are you doing here?" because the last thing I knew he was in Canada. As we went to the hospital, he explained what had happened.

It was a weird thing, not knowing where you are or why your dad is there. It turned out to be a very serious concussion. They took x-rays, and while there were no broken bones, I was very disoriented. They told my dad to wake me up every hour that night, so he stayed awake and followed the instructions. He also set the alarm clock in case he fell asleep. It took two or three days for me to get my wits about me. My equilibrium was off, and I couldn't walk properly. My dad ended up driving me to Kentucky, where I had a few more days off, and I thought I'd be okay. I went out in the morning two or three times to exercise some horses, but I realized I wouldn't be able to ride because I couldn't even focus. I went back to Toronto and visited a doctor who said, "You can't ride again until I say you can ride again." I was off for two months after that spill.

I wanted to be back in the saddle for opening day at Woodbine, in the third week in April. I did start to feel better and was able to meet that target date. We ended up having a good year, finishing first among jockeys with 17 stakes wins and leading the meet with 141 wins from 688 mounts. I had purse earnings of more than $3.6 million. Don Seymour eclipsed my Canadian purse-earnings mark with more than $4.8 million, much of it derived from sweeping the Canadian Triple Crown aboard Kinghaven Farms' With Approval, the first horse to win the three-race series in twenty-six years. Coincidentally, he did it in the first year that the Bank of Montreal offered a million-dollar bonus to a horse that swept the series. (The bonus was withdrawn a couple of years later, after Izvestia and Dance Smartly swept the Triple Crown, making it three winners in three consecutive years. Talk about breaking the bank!)

I had a scheduled mount in the Breeders' Cup in Florida that year, but my horse was scratched during the week because of an injury. I ended up going, and John Tyre joined me. His recollection is that we went out for dinner — eating macrobiotic food, of course. Overall in 1989, we won 151 races from 836 mounts and surpassed $4 million in purse earnings. All and all, considering the riding mishaps, it wasn't a bad year.

* * *

In 1989, my personal life changed significantly. It was the year I met Lisa John, the woman I would later marry and with whom I would start a family. Lisa came into the picture through my longtime friend Dave Westlake, with whom I'd grown up in Oshawa. He became my insurance agent when I moved my investments from California. He used to love coming out to the races; he was a huge racing fan. One day, he came to the track and said, "Sandy, you're not with anyone right now, are you?" No, not at the moment.

"I've got this cute secretary. She's really a nice girl, and I think you might get along really well. She's five-foot-two."

That piqued my interest. I'd never really been out with a girl my size. They'd all been taller than me. So I agreed, and told him to bring her along the next time he came to the track.

The next time he came to the track, there was no secretary to be seen. I joked with him about it: "Hey, where's that cute secretary you said you were going to bring along?" "She was busy this time," he said, "but I'll definitely bring her next time I come." I guess it was about two weeks later that he came out to the track again. I was looking forward to meeting her. Lisa tells the story better than I do, but suffice it to say that Dave twisted her arm to meet me.

Lisa Hawley:
I was really busy one day, when Dave said to me, "I want you to meet somebody. You might really like this guy."

"No," I said, "I don't really want to meet anybody right now. I'm not interested." He insisted: "Lisa, you really should meet him."

"Forget it, Dave. I don't want to meet anybody."

The reason was that I had broken up almost a year before with someone I'd been involved in a four-year relationship with. I wasn't really ready to go out with anybody new. Dave went to see Sandy, and he came back to me the following week and said, "You've got to meet this guy. I promised him you'd meet him."

I stopped in my tracks — I was really upset — and said, "Tell me who it is, but that doesn't mean I'm going to meet him." So he told, and I said, "Sandy Hawley? I don't want to meet him." Mind you, I *had* met Sandy several years prior, when he came to cut the ribbon at our new office. I was engaged to somebody else at the time and he had his second wife with him. He doesn't remember meeting me.

"Why don't you want to meet him?" Dave asked.

"First of all, he's too old. He's too short. He's been married before. And if this guy can't find a girl in Toronto, there's something seriously wrong with him." I live in Oshawa, a small town.

"Listen," he said. "I promised him we'd go up to Woodbine, so on Friday we'll go there — we'll work half a day, go to the races and then go to dinner at his favourite Chinese restaurant and then I'll bring you home."

"Okay, Dave," I said, "but don't ever do that again because it makes me feel awkward. The guy wants to meet me, he may be disappointed. I'm not interested in him anyway."

We went up there — in those days you'd have box seats and you had to pay for parking and you had to get passes to get in — and as Sandy was riding through the tunnel leading to the track for a race, Dave yelled out to him and Sandy waved up to us and said, "Did you get your parking pass okay? Are your seats okay? Is everything all right?" He was just trying to make sure we were settled.

He didn't see me — Dave is a big guy, over six feet and over 200 pounds — and I was impressed. I thought that was really nice. He's going out there and trying to concentrate on what he's going to do for a race, but he's taking the time out — and looking way up — to make sure we were okay getting in. After the races, we met outside the jocks' room and Dave was teasing me: "Look, he's brushing his hair for you. He's phoning his parents to talk about you!"

We went to a Chinese restaurant in Mississauga, and Lisa was on her second plate of food and was cutting into a chicken ball when it slipped. Her plate ended up landing upside down on my lap, all over the pair of khakis I was wearing. I didn't get upset — accidents happen. I just put the plate back up on the table. Lisa said she was impressed that I didn't get upset. I remember it was almost like being on your first date.

Lisa Hawley:
My whole plate just slipped on Sandy's tan-coloured pants. You've got soy sauce, sweet-and-sour chicken-ball sauce, all over his lap. I was shocked. By this time, I'm getting to like this guy. I didn't know what to do. He started scooping up the grains of rice and I was all apologetic. I offered to pay to clean his pants. "Nah, don't worry about it," he said. He was really good about it.

As we were leaving the restaurant, he said, "I guess if I asked you for your phone number, you'd probably say no."

"I don't know," I said. "Why don't you ask and find out?" I gave him my number and we said goodbye.

As Dave drove me home, he asked, "What do you think of him?" I pointed my finger at him and said, "I'm going to marry that guy."

Dave just laughed — his belly jiggled like Santa Claus'. He said, "Why? You've never said that before." But I'd never felt that way about anybody on meeting them the first time. I said to Dave, "Because he's a nice guy and he's sincere."

For the second date, I went up to meet him at Woodbine. We were going from the track to the same Chinese restaurant, and I was following him in my car, and it conked out along the way. I didn't have a cell phone back then and I lost him. All I could do was limp off the highway and find a phone and call the restaurant.

When Sandy got there, he told the waiter the table would be for just one, but the waiter told him I had just called and was on the way. I got there about ten or fifteen minutes later, and he was quite impressed that I had found my way, because I really didn't know Toronto. "For putting you through all this," he said, "I'm going to buy you dinner." I said, "No, I work. There's no reason why I shouldn't be buying *you* dinner. I've always done that for my old boyfriends."

That was really the start of our relationship. He won my heart, and two years later to the month, we got married.

What I didn't recall at the time was that I had actually seen Lisa once before, when I happened to be in Toronto to ride in a race. I had a little bit of spare time, so I stopped off at the grand opening of Dave's office, which was covered by the media. Lisa was there because she worked for Dave, but I don't have any recollection of meeting her that day. But I'll always remember meeting her eleven years later.

* * *

Professionally, 1990 proved to be a bittersweet season. We led the Woodbine meet with 128 wins, twelve of them stakes, from 709 mounts and had purse earnings of more than $3.2 million. I won the Canadian Oaks once more, this time with Sam-Son Farm's Tiffany's Secret. Overall, on the Ontario Jockey Club circuit we led with 142 wins from 768 mounts and had purse earnings of more than $3.7 million, second only to Don Seymour, who swept the Triple Crown for the second season in a row with With Approval's stablemate, Izvestia. But I had lost some of my business with Sam-Son Farm, which had decided to employ Brian Swatuk. We were both on Sam-Son horses in the Breeders' Cup Juvenile Fillies at Belmont Park in New York. I was aboard Dance Smartly, who was considered the best two-year-old filly in the barn, and Brian rode Wilderness Song, who had won back-to-back stakes races going into the Breeders' Cup.

I felt Dance Smartly had a really good chance to win. She had won a stakes race on the grass in her last start, and had three wins and a second on the season. There was another great horse in the race, New York–based Meadow Star, who was undefeated and the big favourite racing on her home ground. When the gate opened up, Dance Smartly almost outbroke the starting gate. She broke so fast, she was almost a length in front, doing it herself. It was very hard for me to try and strangle her and bring (or rate) her back — she was a natural speed horse anyway. Trainer Jim Day thought that Wilderness Song was going to have more speed than Dance Smartly and felt that she should be the one that was on the lead. She ended up showing some speed as well. I think there were three of us going along there for a while.

Normally, in a situation like this, one of the horses in the coupled entry will take back — the two won't battle one another for the lead. I just wanted Dance Smartly to run within herself, instead of fighting with her. With such a long stretch, it is very hard to go wire to wire. Sometimes a rider has to use his own judgement, and I thought I was using mine by not strangling her and taking her back. Dance Smartly tired in the stretch and finished third by six lengths to Meadow Star. If I had won the race, I think things would have been fine, but since I ended up third — when I was expected to come from just off the pace and Wilderness Song was the one that was supposed to show the speed — there was criticism afterward.

Jim Day was a little upset. He didn't show it, but I could tell. He asked me why she was on the lead, and I just said, "She broke so fast that she was a length in front of anybody, just going so easily the whole way, and I used my own judgement and didn't drag her back." I guess Jim Day was under the impression that I should have taken her back. So the writing was on the wall: I lost the mount on Dance Smartly, who would go on to an undefeated season in 1991 and win the Eclipse Award as the top three-year-old filly in North America as well as horse-of-the-year honours in

Canada. She was ridden for her first two starts as a three-year-old by Brian Swatuk, who subsequently lost the mount when he missed a scheduled workout and was replaced by Pat Day. Pat was not related to Jim Day, but he was held in high regard by Jim. I had ridden against Pat Day back when I rode in Chicago in 1986, and he would develop into one of the top riders in North America.

I had hoped to stay on Dance Smartly, but Jim Day had a talk with Mr. Samuel and that's when the decision was made. It was disappointing to lose the mount, but that's part of the business.

Chapter Ten

Lisa and the Kids

In the winter of 1991, I parted with my longtime agent, Colin Wick. Again, it was purely business — nothing personal. Colin and I are great friends now, and looking back on the move it was an unfortunate series of events. Colin had been booking mounts for Mickey Walls, an apprentice rider who had come from British Columbia the previous fall, when I had returned to California, and led the Greenwood meet with 42 wins from 233 mounts. Mickey's father, Joe, who is a trainer, asked Colin to become Mickey's agent. Colin agreed, but the arrangement was only supposed to last until the end of the 1990 season, after which he would work exclusively for me. I was to get married to Lisa in 1991 and I wanted to have a big season, so I was counting on Colin.

But the way Colin was talking to everyone, it sounded like he intended to continue working full time for Mickey. I told Colin, "I feel a little uncomfortable about the situation. You're going to have Mickey, and he's probably going to be one of the top riders. And I want to strive to be leading rider. You said you were only going to have me."

He said he'd changed his mind. "This is bad, Colin," I said. "I just want you to have me." Colin is a very strong-willed person, and I guess I was giving him an ultimatum. "Well," he replied, "I'm going to have Mickey and I'm going to have you, too." I repeated, "No. I just want you to have me."

I was thinking about my interests, because I knew he was the best agent on the grounds, but at the same time I was also concerned for Colin's health. Working for both of us, he seemed stressed. I even tried to convince him that if he worked exclusively for me, he'd have time to go fishing whenever he wanted. It was a tug of war; I stuck to my guns, and he stuck to his. And, of course, it ended up not working out in my favour.

Colin Wick:

I said, "After more than twenty years, you're going to dictate to me what I can and can't do? I don't think that's right."

He said, "I might not be leading rider if you've got Mickey Walls — he might be."

I said, "Sandy, he might be leading rider anyway. He's a talented young rider and he's got the bug. At least if I've got him, I control what's going on. I control what he's doing and I control what you're doing. If I don't have him, any agent that gets him will work against you and me. Who you're listening to, I don't know."

The bottom line was that he threw me an ultimatum, and I said, "After all these years, I don't think I should be dictated to." I thought about it and I said, "No, you're not going to dictate to me. If you want me, you've got me, but you can't tell me what to do. I'm too old for that.

"You're first in line with me," I told him. "Nobody comes before you. I don't know who you're listening to." As far as I'm concerned, he's always number one with me, and I think he would say the same thing. He's like a son to me. Nobody comes before Sandy Hawley, as far as I'm concerned.

I ended up going with Lorne Spearman, who is an excellent agent. He had worked a long time for Irwin Driedger, who retired midway through the following year to become the secretary/manager of the Jockeys' Benefit Association of Canada. Irwin had once ridden first call for Sam-Son Farm, and his last career race was aboard Dance Smartly in her first lifetime race. I continued to ride occasionally for Sam-Son, but Mickey started riding quite a lot for the outfit. Colin was good friends with Jim Day, and not having Colin plugging for me hurt my chances as well.

On the marriage front, Lisa and I had picked June 17 as our wedding date and Oshawa — where I was born and raised — as the place where we would have the ceremony. I'm nine years older than Lisa, and I've always wondered if I had ever seen her on the street. It would have been pretty funny if I had, and if I'd caught a glimpse of the future and been able to say to her, "Little girl, one of these days I'm going to marry you."

Once, I went to Trinidad to ride in a jockey challenge — it was about a year and a half after we had married — and I spun a variation on that story to a newspaper reporter. And he printed it! Lisa's uncle came up to her and said, "I can't believe that when you were seven years old, Sandy came up and said that to you." And we said, "No, no, no! It was just a story we made up." He was fooled for a little while, though.

Lisa Hawley:
I didn't chase him — we just dated. And the whole while he kept saying to me, "I'm not getting married again. I'm not getting married again." I said, "I've never once mentioned the 'M' word to you. What makes you think I want to marry you?"

I never heard him mention marriage again until he proposed to me. I figured, "If he wants to marry me, he'll ask me." I wasn't dating anybody. I was having a good time with him. I thought, "I'm a big girl. If it doesn't work out, fine. He told me he's not going to get married, that's okay. I'm not going to make anybody marry me. In the meantime, we're having a good time. I'll face the music down the road if I have to get hurt or whatever."

But we did get married. I've often thought to myself, I must have done something good in life, because God gave me Sandy. He's the nicest person I know.

My dad stood up for me as my best man. At the time, I had a lot of good friends, but none I could really single out as my best friend. And I just felt that I loved my dad and I wanted him to be my best man. I asked Colin to be in the wedding party. That's the funny thing: we were supposed to be on the outs, but we were still friends, and he accepted the offer.

There was quite a cross-section of individuals at the wedding, including retired hockey player Reggie Fleming, whom I knew from my days riding in Chicago; Marty McSorley of the Los Angeles Kings; National Hockey League referee Andy Van Hellemond; Gerry Gallitano, the jockey I lived with when I rode in Chicago (he was also in our wedding party); Bill Meuris, who had hired me to work in the penalty box at Los Angeles Kings home games; my California valet, Jack Wood; and my longtime California-based friend John Tyre, who accompanied Jack on the plane.

Oddly enough, because I was riding year-round, I never had a full honeymoon after any of my three weddings. I can't remember where we went the first two times, but when I married Lisa we went up north for a few days to the Deerhurst Inn in Huntsville. It was not far from where my uncle, Ed Keetch, had his cottage — where I'd gone as a youth growing up in Oshawa. Uncle Ed came by the resort and had a drink with Lisa and me. They had some entertainment at the resort, which we really enjoyed, and believe it or not, we went horseback riding there.

Lisa had only been riding once before, and on that occasion her horse tried to take off on her. I gave her the ins and outs of how to hold the reins. Lisa was impressed because I was in front, taking pictures while I rode. The guy who looked after the horse recognized me, which was kind of neat, but fortunately he didn't give me the wildest horse in the barn. Or maybe he did… when you go to a ranch like that, even the wildest one isn't that wild.

Lisa and I bought a house in Mississauga, and I had a decent season, finishing third in wins with 103 from 667 mounts and earning purses worth more than $2.5 million. Overall, I finished with 116 wins from 823 mounts and more than $2.8 million in purses. With Colin's guidance, Mickey Walls finished as the Canadian leader in wins, with 285 from 1,313 mounts, and set a record with more than $5.5 million in purse earnings. He became the first rider to a win Sovereign Awards as top apprentice and top journeyman in the same year. He also won an Eclipse Award as top apprentice. He lost his apprentice allowance on the same day he erased my record of 230 wins by a Canadian-based apprentice. He also broke my mark of 190 wins at Woodbine.

* * *

I came into 1992 preparing for the birth of our first child. When Lisa and I first became serious, she had said she wanted children if she ever married. When I proposed to her, I put it this way: "Will you marry me and become the mother of my children?" We knew at that point we were going to try and have a family. And we didn't waste any time: she became pregnant a month after we were married. You never know exactly what date the delivery will be, but a week before the due date I said, "Please try and have it on a Monday — my day off." And if you can believe it, she went into the hospital on a Monday — though she had the baby the following day, May 5. I ended up riding the next night.

We didn't know ahead of time if it was going to be a boy or a girl. Lisa was well into her labour, and she was really suffering, when I said to her, "If you give me a boy, you won't have to go through this again." She gave me a look like she was going to strangle me! But she had a boy, whom we named Bradley Desmond. I always liked the name Bradley. If it was a girl it was going to be Britney Anna. Lisa's sister-in-law later had a girl and named her Britney.

Being a father and holding my own baby in my arms came so naturally to me, which was a surprise, because any time I'd ever held a baby before, I just felt like I was going to break it. I have a godson, Nicholas Gigone, whose parents, Franco and Janet Gigone, I became good friends with in Fort Erie. When Nicholas was a baby, I felt so uncomfortable holding him. But when Bradley was born and they put him in my arms, it was almost like I was cradling a football — no problem at all. Fatherhood ended up coming very naturally to me. I thought I'd have to change, be something I wasn't, but I found out early on that you just have to be yourself.

In August, I was inducted into the National Museum of Racing Hall of Fame. I had been on the ballot for two or three years before that, and to finally be selected was tremendous. Being in the Canadian Horse Racing Hall of Fame was enough of a thrill, but to go into the North American one was unbelievable. My parents came to the induction ceremony at

Saratoga, along with Lisa and a contingent from the Ontario Jockey Club: president Jack Kenney, vice president of racing John Whitson and publicity director Bruce Walker.

To introduce me, I chose *Daily Racing Form* executive columnist Joe Hirsch, who was also the Hall of Fame committee chairman, and I was very pleased when he accepted. He summarized my numerous racing achievements, then talked about me as a person:

> Sandy Hawley is more than a rider of winners. He has conducted himself in a gentlemanly fashion since his first day at the track. He is one of the few men honoured by his colleagues in two countries for personifying the highest standards of his profession. He has been honoured with the Avelino Gomez Award in Canada and the George Woolf Memorial Award in the United States. He exemplifies grace under pressure and has the admiration of the entire racing community.

Joe had done a number of articles on me, and had always been very kind to me in them. I recall the very first time he was going to interview me. I was a little bit late — I had been doing morning workouts and the interview had simply skipped my mind. Somebody said, "I saw Joe Hirsch in the kitchen, and he said he was supposed to do an interview with you this morning." I was mortified; I knew Joe Hirsch and how important he was — and here I was, just a young apprentice. I was very upset to have missed my appointment with him; I called the *Form* and I was very apologetic. I actually mentioned in my acceptance speech that I made it a point never to miss another appointment with Joe Hirsch.

* * *

My mother was not feeling well, and for a whole year the doctors couldn't figure out what was ailing her. When Bradley was being christened, my dad came from Fort Erie alone because my mom couldn't make it. We hadn't seen her in about a month, during which she had really gone downhill.

"She's in bed," my dad said. "She's not well." Lisa vowed that we would go pay her a visit the next weekend. When we got there, she was on her deathbed. We took one look at her and said to my dad, "We're taking her to the hospital in Mississauga, because she does not look good at all." She was kind of in and out of it; she was awake, but you could tell by her eyes that she wasn't there.

We brought her back to Mississauga and went to the emergency room. They looked her over and planned to keep her overnight. I thought they would admit her, because she looked that bad. I went to ride the next day, and when I came home, Mom was there. "What's going on here?" I asked. I ended up calling my valet, Ronnie Robinson, who had the same family doctor as us, Nancy Austin. Ronnie and his wife, Jackie, suggested that we call Dr. Austin and see if we could get my mom admitted to the hospital. Dr. Austin told us to bring my mother back to the emergency room, where she examined Mom immediately had her readmitted. That evening, Dr. Austin called to say my mother had gone into a coma. "We're going to have to perform emergency surgery. We don't know what's wrong with her," Dr. Austin said.

They didn't even think she'd make it through surgery, but they operated. Lisa, my dad and I waited in the chapel, where we cried and prayed for her. When we were allowed to see her, we counted sixteen tubes and bottles attached to her. The doctors said they'd discovered she had Crohn's Disease, and that if we had waited just two days, she wouldn't have made it. Crohn's Disease causes inflammation in the intestine and it can be difficult to diagnose because its symptoms are similar to other intestinal disorders.

Mom had always wanted a grandchild, and I'd got to a point where I thought I'd never have a child. When my mom first met Lisa, she told me, "If you ever give me any grandchildren, I hope it's with Lisa." She was giving Lisa a big boost. My mother was tough on every woman I'd gone out with — probably because I was an only child — but it was just the opposite with Lisa. She really did love her, and when we had our first child, my mother adored Bradley so much. She bought him his first wagon and planned to do many things with him, but she was so sick she could hardly lift and hold him. Still, she was so proud of him. I remember her going to see some of her sisters and brothers with Bradley, and at this point she was so sick that she couldn't even keep anything down. She still wanted to take Bradley for the weekend, to be able to go to all the relatives and show off her new grandson.

I rode the full Greenwood meet for the first time in sixteen years, and in November I recorded my 6,000th career win aboard a horse called Summer Commander. The horse was trained by Bob Tiller, who had saddled the 3,000th winner of my career, also at Greenwood. It was just a tremendous thrill. Dad was there, and so was Lisa with her family. I had a picture taken of myself with Lisa and Bradley, who was about six months old. In the days leading up to the historic win, Lisa had been coming to the races with her brothers, sisters and parents, not wanting to miss it.

Lisa Hawley:
I brought Bradley to the track, and he had no idea what was going on because he was only a few months old, but it was very special. It was a cold, dark evening, and Sandy had said, "Just be ready. I want you guys to be there in the winner's circle for the picture." I said, "No problem. We'll be there, don't worry about us. If we're late coming down, it's because it's cold and I'll be carrying the baby. Just hold off and wait for us, and we'll be in the picture." Sure enough, he did, and it was wonderful to share that with him and to have Bradley there. It was great.

We finished the season with 99 wins from 713 mounts and had purse earnings of just under $2.9 million.

In 1993, my season ended in October when I went into hospital to have a malignant tumour surgically removed from one of my lungs. I was actually in the same hospital, Mount Sinai, as my mother. I remember telling her, "Maybe we'll both get out at the same time." But she spent more time in the hospital than out of it.

The spot had been there for three or four years, and Dr. Malcolm Mitchell, the California oncologist who had started me on the immune therapy vaccine program, said at the outset that he hadn't been too concerned about it because tumours like that one don't spread from the lung when it's melanoma. He said he would just keep monitoring it and keep up the vaccine, and with any luck it would go away. I was taking the vaccine twice at year at that point, after having originally taken it once a month. That made for some hectic times, because when I was in Chicago, I was riding six days a week, so on my one day off I would fly all the way to California to get my vaccine and then fly straight back.

The tumour was growing at a very slow pace, but Dr. Lou Teglas, the on-site doctor on the Ontario Jockey Club circuit for many years — and who became my family doctor — kept an eye on it for me as well. I was going for CAT scans and x-rays every six months, and he noticed that it was getting bigger and suggested that we should do something about it. He called Dr. Mitchell in California and had a talk with him, and Dr. Mitchell concluded that Dr. Teglas should go ahead and take it out. The tumour ended up being about the size of a golf ball.

At the time I had the surgery, we had 46 wins from 437 mounts and purse earnings of almost $1.5 million.

My mother passed away in December. Her illness had just gone so far that it was impossible to save her. Lisa was four months pregnant with our second child, Russell, when my mother died. We were very upset that Mom couldn't spend more time with Bradley, or live long enough to see Russell. They're good boys, and she would have been very proud of them.

Because I was an only child, I dreaded losing one of my parents. It was so tough when she became ill and it looked as if she was going to die, and then to see her come out of it and struggle to stay alive — it was a battle. We always held out hope that she was going to get better. The night she passed away, Lisa and I had left the hospital room before my dad. There was a boxing match on that night, and I told my dad we'd watch it when he came home. He arrived about an hour after I'd left, and he said my mother had told him, "Don't leave,

Des. Don't leave." Maybe she knew something, because she passed away that evening. We got the phone call and went back to the hospital. I remember that as if was yesterday.

In 1994, I rode in California in the winter and also went to Barbados for a few days to ride in the Cockspur Gold Cup, the premier race in the British West Indies, and won with a horse called Chou Chou Royale.

Lisa Hawley:
It was the proudest moment of my life, watching Sandy ride in that race. Even though he'd won big stakes races — I wasn't in his life when he won those Queen's Plates and Canadian Oaks. When we were in Barbados and I watched him take a 13–1 nutbar and come riding down the stretch, I thought about what a magnificent rider he is. He showed his true talent.

He was patient on a horse, he waited for the right time and he made his move. That horse was mean and vicious and big. You couldn't even take a picture in the winner's circle with her — she was that bad. When he won with her, I couldn't believe it. I thought, "What a talent this guy has!"

The horse was owned by David Seale, who owns a prominent rum company in the islands and was later knighted by Queen Elizabeth. Lisa became good friends with David's daughter-in-law, who is from Toronto. The trip was set up by Ralph Boissiere, a writer for one of the Trinidad newspapers. I'd met him a couple years before, when I rode in Trinidad in a competition, and he became my agent for the islands. We also went to Puerto Rico to ride, although at the last second my horse took sick and had to be scratched.

On the home front, Lisa and I celebrated the birth of our second child when Russell was born on April 18. I knew the age difference between the two boys would be perfect, and hoped that they would become buddies, which they did. We chose the name Russell because Lisa and I both have favourite cousins by that name. Before he was born, I didn't care whether it was a boy or a girl as long as it was healthy. I think every parent feels the same way. It was fantastic having another child, and, given that it was a boy, it was just like having Bradley all over again. When Russell was born, it was a little more comfortable for me. I wasn't as nervous, and I knew I would be able to help Lisa out — I knew that I could be strong for her. I was still nervous, hoping everything would work out okay, but afterwards, when it was clear he was born healthy and happy, I was more at ease.

CHAPTER ELEVEN

The Final Years

We had a good year in my comeback season of 1994, recording 153 wins from 859 mounts and placing third in purse earnings with more than $2.5 million. We won seven stakes races, one of them with Terremoto, a horse who would become important personally at the end of my career.

Heading into 1995, I felt great. I was leading the Ontario Jockey Club standings when my season came to a sudden halt after the most serious racing mishap of my career. It was early in the card on Wednesday evening, August 2, and my horse, Regent's Revenue, was walking in the post parade in front of the grandstand. The horse in front of mine backed into Regent's Revenue, who reared up to get out of the way, falling over backwards. When I landed on the ground, I thought I was okay because I've had that happen before — you go one way and the horse goes the other — but unfortunately the horse landed right on top of me and then rolled off of me. She weighed about 1,200 pounds — on the heavy side for thoroughbreds, who average about 1,000 pounds or so — and after she rolled off of me it felt like a chiropractor had just adjusted every single bone in my body.

It was by far the worst accident of my career. The full extent of my injuries wasn't immediately apparent, but it would be discovered that I had broken my pelvis, shattered a vertebra, severed my urethra (which is the urinary tract), dislocated my left shoulder and broken two ribs on my left side.

When the paramedic came to tend to me, he said, "Where does it hurt?" He knew I was in bad shape. I replied, "My back is hurting bad, and the worst pain I have right now is right in the middle of my asshole." I think I kind of laughed a little bit, and I gave him a little bit of a giggle, but in fact I was in a great deal of pain. The proof is that I don't usually swear. I also told him I had a stinging sensation in my penis, not even knowing I had a severed urethra.

Lisa Hawley:

I got a phone call from Ronnie Robinson, Sandy's former valet, who was working at the time as the paddock judge. — I dreaded those calls. He said, "Lisa, I've got something to tell you."

"No," I said.

"Sandy's at Etobicoke General."

Sandy's car was at the track, and I felt I couldn't leave it there for days. I told Ronnie, "I'm too upset to drive," and he said, "Don't worry. I'll send over John (his son-in-law, who lived around the corner) and he'll get you and bring you to the track. Just take the car over to Etobicoke General and I'll be there."

I asked him what was wrong with Sandy, and he didn't think it was anything serious, maybe a broken rib or something.

Ronnie Robinson:

I knew that he was injured quite badly, but I wasn't going to tell Lisa that. It's bad enough to hear that he's hurt, but I wouldn't want to let on that he's hurt real bad. You don't want to say how bad you think it is because you can't make a call for something like that.

I was pretty sure his pelvic bone was broken. Anytime you get one of them, that's major. What's going to come of it, you don't know.

I wanted to tell her that he was hurt and that we'd make sure she got to the hospital, but I didn't want her to think that it was really bad and start fretting right away.

I've seen jocks go down, and you'd think they could get up and walk away, but they've really broken both their legs. And other jocks look like they've gotten killed and they'd just get up and walk away.

Lisa Hawley:

I left the kids at home with my sister-in-law and got to the hospital. The waiting room was full of racetrackers: Irwin Driedger, the secretary/manager of the Jockeys' Benefit Association of Canada; Sandy's agent, Mike Langlais; Hugh Blackmore, the owner of the horse that landed on him; his daughter; and the trainer of the horse, Brad Dunslow. It was just packed, and I was really upset.

I get in to see Sandy, and he said he was in a lot of pain. I said, "Tell me about it. What's happening?" He said, "I'm in a lot of pain and I've got this gurgling sound. I've never had it before." He said the doctors had looked at it and thought it was only a bruised or cracked rib, but Sandy said he'd hurt his ribs before and this time it felt different.

They were really busy in emergency, but I asked them to look at Sandy again. They kept brushing me off, and I got really upset because Sandy kept saying that there was something wrong with him. I went to the doctor in charge and said, "Somebody better listen to me because I've got a husband out there who never complains about anything. When he tells me there's something wrong with him, there *is*, so you'd better look at him right now. I've been waiting here for hours and I'm not prepared to wait any longer. If I have to, there's going to be repercussions to this. I am not kidding here. I know there's other people you've been tending to, but I think this is something serious, and I think he deserves priority treatment."

They looked at me, and I felt like a real witch, but I thought I've been waiting here for hours and they've been brushing this off and there *is* something wrong.

It was pretty scary. At the time, I wasn't sure if my career was over or not, but I did know I had something seriously wrong with me. Because I was in so much pain, I had a feeling that I would be out for a long time. I'd had accidents before, but I knew this one was very significant. At about midnight, the visitors were told that I had a few bruises and that I'd be off for a period of time, but everything would be all right. That was enough to convince all those people who had come by the hospital that they could go home. But I kept telling Lisa I still heard the gurgling sound and that it was concerning me. After Lisa became angry with the hospital staff, they decided to inject some dye into my penis, take an x-ray, and find out if there was a problem.

A little while later, they came back and said they didn't know where the dye went — it didn't show up on the x-ray — so they had to perform emergency surgery. They told Lisa that they would call her if she wanted to go home, but Lisa wouldn't leave. She wanted to be there when I came out of surgery. I started having flashbacks to Avelino Gomez's death on the operating table in 1980 after suffering internal injuries in the Canadian Oaks.

Lisa Hawley:
I took a chair and sat quiet as could be in the hallway outside the operating room. It was pitch dark except for a coffee machine. I can't remember how long it was, but they came out and said Sandy had a broken pelvis, shattered vertebrae, a severed urethra, three or four cracked ribs and a dislocated shoulder. I saw him when he came out; he had tubes attached to him. They said they had fixed everything and that he was fine. I made sure after seeing him that everything was satisfactory, then I went home. It was about five in the morning, and I lay down and got up around seven and was back at the hospital by nine. My sister-in-law and my mother looked after the kids.

I was in the intensive-care unit for a few days. They gave me morphine for the pain. I called Lou Teglas, our family doctor, and he arranged to ship me across town to Sunnybrook Hospital. We thought that was the best place for me, because Sunnybrook has a trauma unit. I was there for three weeks and then, when I was able to move much better, I was transferred to Credit Valley Hospital, which was closer to our home. I was there for about two weeks, then I went home and recuperated for about two months.

In all, I was sidelined for eight months. I had tubes for my urethra for more than five months, and I needed to use crutches for that period of time because of my broken pelvis. When I needed something, I would bang on the floor with my crutches. Here's Lisa, with a three-year-old son and another that's not even a year and a half, and I'm the biggest baby of them all!

Lisa Hawley:
I was never so tired in all my life.

He had tubes coming out of him — to this day he has a second belly button from one of those tubes. He was on medication for pain and for healing — and he had a catheter and I had to change the bag. I had to get him up in the morning and sponge bathe him in the bed and give him his medication and his breakfast.

I had young kids, including one who was fourteen months and barely walking, and I had to get them up. I'd just be finished feeding them and then have to run upstairs to take care of him. He couldn't really move in bed — he was a bit of an invalid. He would lie on one part of his shoulder and it would get sore and he couldn't take the pain.

Because it was a big house, I couldn't hear him call me from way downstairs, so I told him, "Just bang the crutches on the ground and I'll hear you." I'd come upstairs and turn him over on one side or empty his bag or give him his medication — sometimes I'd get so busy I'd forget about giving it to him. I'd have all these medications to give him — and he was slowly weaning off certain things. Sometimes he just needed to have his head lifted because he really was banged up a lot.

Eventually I brought in a physiotherapist, and she worked on moving him around and giving him exercise. That helped me out a lot, too.

He really didn't complain a lot to me. All he'd say is, "Lisa, my bag needs changing" or "I've got to go to the toilet." He'd have to lean all his weight on me — and I'm not that big — and get on the toilet. Then I'd have to get him dressed and back in bed, or feed him, because his shoulder was hurt so bad.

Every day it was the same routine. Get up and look after him and the kids. It was tiring. When I hit the sack at night, I was exhausted. I just crashed. I didn't want morning to come. It would feel like I'd just gone to bed, and two hours later I'd wake up and think, "Oh, no, here we go again." As time went on, we didn't need the physiotherapist anymore, so I would stretch out Sandy's neck or help out with his leg. He would get really bad headaches from the pain in the shoulder and the ribs. He'd lean one way and go, "Ow" and lean the other way and be sore. The broken pelvis gave him a lot of pain, too.

My mom and dad and brothers and sisters came over so I could get a good night's rest — everybody chipped in. They were great. My family was just wonderful.

After about a month, I got him downstairs in the family room and put him in the La-Z-Boy chair so he could recline and watch TV and just be with us — just get a change of scenery from the bedroom. One day, he was sitting there and the tears came streaming down his face. I asked him, "What's the matter?" He said, "I just feel so helpless. I'm tired of being in pain and seeing you running around like crazy looking after the kids and I can't help you with the house or anything else. I feel like a burden to you." I said, "You're not a burden. Don't feel terrible. Just get yourself better. Don't worry about me. I can handle it."

Because of Sandy's severed urethra, the doctor didn't know if he would ever be able to have sex again. I told Sandy, "That doesn't matter to me. That's nothing. I can live with that. I love you, we've got two kids together, and we have a great life. If that's the worst that can happen, it doesn't matter. Life goes on. You're not going to lose me. I'm going to be here for you." He just cried — which he normally would never do — and let out all that tension, all that pain, all that anxiety, the frustration. Then he felt better.

I said, "I'm there for you. You'd do the same for me. We're a team and we'll get through this. I don't ever want to hear you say anything else like that again. Just get better and we'll be okay."

He said, "How are we doing financially?"

"Fine," I said. "We've got a nest egg and besides that we're doing great, so don't worry. Everything is taken care of." We *were* doing okay — we had money put away. I let him know he didn't have to worry about anything because I looked after all the financial stuff.

Slowly, I reached the point where I was able to get around with my crutches. I'd go out to the mall — the colostomy bag from my catheter hidden under my clothes — and I'd hobble around. I was slowly becoming independent. Eventually, I no longer needed Lisa to help me up and down the stairs — she'd stand at the bottom in case I fell back or slipped, but she let me do my own thing because I was very strong-willed about that.

After six months, everything was healing well and I decided to go to California to get back into riding shape. The doctors didn't want me to get on a horse until the spring, but I felt well enough to try. I told Lisa I thought I could do it, and she just told me not to push myself too hard. So, we packed and took the kids to California. I started getting on a few horses in the mornings. I was so stiff and sore, because I'd never been away for that long.

By the time I made my comeback, I had only exercised three horses. In my first race, I rode a horse called Diamond Lane, a 30–1 shot, and finished second-last. I really felt pretty sore afterward. My legs were burning and I was having trouble catching my breath. I was stiff and sore the next day, too. I continued to exercise horses in the morning and rode the mechanical horse simulator in the jockeys' room during the races, switching my whip from hand to hand as if I was actually riding in the race. I got in shape more quickly than I'd anticipated, and was ready for the opening of the Woodbine season in the third week of March. Given the length of time that had elapsed since the accident, I worried that I might regress in terms of muscle loss, but I really didn't. As for riding again, I felt almost like I was starting all over again. But it's kind of like riding a bike: you just jump back on, and a week later it's like old times again.

In 1996, the Breeders' Cup came to Woodbine, the first time the event had ever been run outside of the United States. In all my years of riding, I had always been very proud of Woodbine — I used to take brochures with me wherever I went, just to show everyone we had great racing in Canada — so it was a great thrill to have the Breeders' Cup there. I thought the Breeders' Cup would be great for Woodbine, because it would attract out-of-town spectators and show them what Canadian racing was all about. And the event would be televised internationally, so all my friends would be able to see the track for which I had so much affection.

I ended up with two mounts: Runaway Mary in the Juvenile Fillies and Chief Bearhart in the Turf. Both were longshots — Runaway Mary went postward at 56–1 and Chief Bearhart, whom I had ridden locally for Sam-Son Farm and its new trainer, Mark Frostad, was 20–1. Still, it was exciting to have a couple of mounts in such an important event in Woodbine's history.

We really lucked out with the weather. On the day of the races, it was about 15 degrees Celsius, or 60 degrees Fahrenheit. It was a real break, because the weather leading up to the Breeders' Cup day had been cold and damp. All the jockeys who rode in the Breeders' Cup that year were issued long-sleeved mock turtlenecks because it was thought that the weather would be cool. As it turned out, it was too warm to wear them. Well, they ended up being great keepsakes.

Neither of my mounts hit the board. Runaway Mary ran sixth by fifteen lengths, while Chief Bearhart ran eleventh by almost eleven lengths. A year later, Chief Bearheart developed into one of the top distance grass horses in North America; he ended up winning the Breeders' Cup with New York–based Jose Santos, who had become his regular rider.

In 1996, I had 94 wins, nine of them in stakes races, on the Woodbine circuit and purse earnings of more than $2.5 million. I ranked fifth overall among the local jockeys in wins and sixth in purse earnings. About this time, I first began to think about retiring. I'd ridden for almost thirty years. When I came back after the 1995 accident, a few people were honourable and good to me, but it seemed almost like I was starting all over again. So many outfits that I had ridden for before didn't use me right off the bat, and it was very frustrating. I was never going to be the leading rider again, and it was never the same. I just got to the point where I thought I wanted to do something else.

Racing wasn't as exciting for me as it had been in the past. I'd talked about it before with Lisa, and she had wanted me to continue riding because she enjoyed watching me ride. So did the kids; Lisa would take them to the track, and they loved visiting the jockeys' room, which had a pool table and a Ping Pong table. Bradley walked in there like he owned the place, and Russell really enjoyed it, too. They loved to climb aboard the tram that took the riders back to the jockeys' room after each race. My valet, Billy O'Connor, would hold Bradley or Russell and I'd hold the other. On one occasion, Lisa was busy, so I took the boys to the track myself. I only had a few races that day, and had some time off in between; while I was out on the track, Billy gave me a hand with the kids. Mainly, they just stood in my stall and waited for me.

Lisa Hawley:
I said, "You know what, Sandy? I'm really selfish. I've always admired your riding over the years, and now, being personally involved, you make me so proud. You're really talented, you're so good at it and we all enjoy watching you so much. I can't see you throwing that talent away and hanging it up, but if you really want to do something else, it's really selfish of me to hold you back from doing what you want. If that's what you really want to do, I'm willing to go along with whatever you want, but if you're not happy, promise me you'll go back and give it a try."

I thought about being a steward or a trainer, but Lisa suggested that I try working in media relations for the Ontario Jockey Club. After all, I'd been used to giving interviews, and I had a good relationship with the public. I thought about it, and it seemed like a great idea. I decided to talk to David Willmot, the president and chief executive officer of the Ontario Jockey Club, and George Hendrie, who was the chairman. I went in to see them, and I told them, "I'm thinking about retiring from riding, and I'd like to know if there would be a position for me."

David Willmot:
Back when we were first making an application to the Canadian Radio-television and Telecommunications Commission (CRTC) for a horse-racing channel, we had put together a team of lawyers and consultants, and Sandy went with us so he could talk about his experiences. I remember the whole day's proceedings were half an hour late in starting because all the members of the CRTC wanted to come down and shake Sandy's hand, talk to him and get his autograph.

Here were these big cable companies, like Rogers and Shaw, sitting in the room, and we're holding up the whole show because Sandy Hawley's there. I remember that had a real impact on me. I knew Sandy was well known, well respected and popular, but it was really interesting to see the reactions of the commission. I think that because I was so affected by that appearance, when he came in and asked if there would be a job here for him, my reaction was immediate.

We get approaches all the time from people who used to ride or maybe wanted to get out of training, and there's just not much there in the way of employment. But Sandy is such a great ambassador — so articulate, so well liked and so respected — I knew there would be a spot for him here. We were thinking at the time more in terms of having him work with our PR department, going out to schools, Rotary clubs, basically taking about his experiences in the industry and drumming up interest in the sport for people of all ages. And he's been fantastic in that.

As our TV department expanded [with the horse-racing channel], Sandy became a key element. We had him work with a consultant in terms of presence on TV — how to articulate, how to ask questions, how to conduct interviews — and he's just matured incredibly well and become a very good commentator.

I was thinking about retiring in 1998, just after the Queen's Plate. The first thing to do was to talk to Glenn Crouter, who was the director of media communications for both the thoroughbred and standardbred divisions, and he told me he was looking forward to having me join the media department as a goodwill ambassador.

Glenn Crouter:
David knew what a classy guy Sandy was, and he said to me, "He'll be perfect for us. We need somebody like Sandy Hawley right now. How would you like to work with him?"

I said, "Wow, you've got to be kidding me. How do you tell a Hall of Famer what to do or how to do it?" It was my second year working at Woodbine, and that's why I was so overwhelmed when I heard it. Sandy could have worked in anybody's department, but he picked ours. For a guy just two years into his job to be working with Sandy Hawley, I considered it an honour that David would think I could work with Sandy and get things done and give him some direction.

David said, "He'll be great. Just give him guidance and everything will work out tremendously."

They told me that, if I wanted to finish out the year, I could begin working for the company the following spring. So I finished out the season, recording 40 wins, seven of them in stakes, from 336 mounts, racking up purse earnings of just under $1.4 million. During that winter, David Gorman, the vice president of corporate affairs at the Ontario Jockey Club

(OJC), sent me to California to talk to the officials at Santa Anita and Del Mar about simulcasting their racing signal for another season.

Glenn Crouter:
You just don't hop off a horse and start into the business world. It's very difficult. He needed a transition. And of course the first year I remember Sandy going to everything. My goal was to get him out to as many places and be exposed to as many people as possible — not only for our benefit, but for his as well. As he got to know more people, and they got to know him, they'd walk away and say, "What a wonderful guy. This guy does not appear to be a legend. This guy does not come off as a superstar. This guy comes off as a real person."

That was the kind of the goal I had in mind when I met him right at the beginning. It's great to get Sandy Hawley in your department, but how can I use him best for everybody — and himself? I thought if we exposed him to as many people as possible, they'd just fall in love with the guy.

Glenn Crouter met with me about when it would be a good time for me to retire. The OJC wanted to make a big deal of it; that's when Glenn came up with the idea of doing it on Canada Day, July 1.

Glenn Crouter:
He's done so much for Canada riding around the world, and with his ambassadorship and his charity work, it just made sense to do it on that day. He's probably one of the best-known athletes in Canada, and it just made sense for him to retire on Canada's birthday.

I agreed it would be a great idea, as a Canadian and a proud one, to retire on Canada Day. I also had a chance to hook up again with Colin Wick that last year, but he didn't want me to ride a lot out of concern for my safety.

Colin Wick:
All I wanted was for Sandy to get through the year without having an accident. I said, "Don't ride much. I'm not going to put you on much." I would hate like hell to see him get hurt, so I told him, "You'll only be riding a few before you retire. You don't need to ride that much." I was afraid of something happening. I would have been really upset and hurt. So he didn't ride much.

I was invited to the National Thoroughbred Racing Association's All-Star Jockey Challenge at Lone Star Park in Texas on June 19, less than two weeks before my retirement. The other jockeys invited included Gary Stevens, Kent Desormeaux, Jerry Bailey, Pat Day, Eddie Delahoussaye, Julie Krone, Chris McCarron, Laffit Pincay, Shane Sellers, Mike Smith and Lone Star's top jockey, Marlon St. Julien. Shane Sellers won. I think I finished somewhere in the middle of the pack — it was just an honour to be invited.

The day I retired was very emotional. The OJC really promoted it heavily. They set up a lavish luncheon in the Post Parade Room and invited my family, relatives and friends, as well as the media. They also had a special cake made up — Lisa said she'd never seen such a big cake. It took up a whole table.

Lisa Hawley:
Leading up to that day was very emotional, very sad. To me, it was the end of a great era. There are great jockeys at Woodbine, don't get me wrong, but Sandy's got a special talent and I was really sad to see the doors finally close on that. But I know he was really looking forward to it because he was enjoying the new job. We were gearing up for it.

Glenn Crouter:
It was Woodbine's gift to Sandy Hawley to say, "Thank you very much, and we look forward to working with you for many years to come." The cake was huge. We

had probably about 300 people from all walks of life. It was only fitting what Woodbine did this for him, because he had done so much for Woodbine. Some people took a piece of cake home — like it was a piece of a wedding cake as a memento. It was like, "I was at Sandy Hawley's last dinner and here's the cake to prove it." Where they would put it, I'm not sure.

The OJC produced a video commemorating my career. The betting vouchers had the words "Sandy's Day" printed on them. There were also giveaways. The OJC printed up a poster of me, with pictures from throughout my career, and the plan was for me to autograph them for a couple hours before I rode. Well, it turned into about three and a half hours because of the lineups. But I couldn't complain; in fact, signing all those autographs kind of took my mind off everything and kept me from being overcome with emotion.

After I was finally done with the autograph session, I only had about an hour to go before my final race. Going into the jockeys' room, seeing the riders and knowing that you're just going out for one last ride was emotional. My last mount was on a horse called Terremoto, whom I had ridden several times before for trainer Beverly Buck. As I was given a leg up on the horse, Lisa said to me, "Go get 'em and just come home safe." It was something she had also said earlier in the day. My mother used to say that to me — "Go get 'em" — before a race, or if she was talking to me on the telephone about a race.

Lisa Hawley:
His mother and I were very close, and it saddened me that she couldn't be there. I always thought of her. So, in her memory, I said, "Go get 'em."

If the first part of Lisa's message was inspired by my mother, the second half was all hers. Lisa and I had been together about ten years by this time, and I had been in nine or ten different hospitals. She came to realize how dangerous the sport is. She used to be afraid, whenever the phone rang, that it might be someone calling to say, "Pick up Sandy at the hospital" or "See Sandy in the hospital." She would just assume that if the phone rang it would be bad news.

Lisa Hawley:
I was there at the jocks' room, and there must have been about twenty-five or thirty cameramen taking pictures. People were coming up to him and wishing him well, and I was just smiling, but deep down inside my heart was breaking because I thought, "I'll never see him ride again. Never. Ever." I was just trying to savour the moment, but I was really upset, too. But I didn't want him to know.

He said, "I'm up against the competition in the race. I'll try my best. I don't know how I'll do." I said, "Just come home safe. Just make it around safe. I don't care. If you win, that's fantastic. Who wouldn't mind ending their career on a winning note, but it doesn't matter. Just come around safe, that's all I want you to do."

On the way to the racetrack, so many people were saying nice things, wishing me well. It put a lump in my throat and brought a tear to my eye.

Terremoto was the type of horse who didn't like to be on the inside; he got frustrated if he couldn't get out early. As luck would have it, I had the number two post position. I wanted to get him to the outside and make my run; unfortunately, they boxed me in the whole way. I did get out midway down the stretch, but it was too late. I ended up finishing third. Mickey Walls won with a horse called Stephanotis.

I'd have loved to win my last race, but at the same time it was very emotional and very exciting to be in that race. It was one of the most vivid memories of my career.

Lisa Hawley:
My dad, the two boys and I stood by the rail and watched him. Russell was crying, "Daddy didn't win, Daddy didn't win." The boys knew it was their dad's last race, so of course they wanted him to win. They'd seen

the press around, and all of the hype; they'd been up in the dining room, and they knew the party, the food, and all of the guests were there because of their dad.

I had to tell Russell, "It doesn't matter. It's okay. Daddy did good. Be happy for Daddy. Daddy doesn't want to see a long face. It will upset him. It's a good day for Daddy." But I wanted him to win, too. It would have been a great note to go out on. He did his best. He got blocked in. They didn't give him a break. They put the squeeze on him. He had nowhere to go with his horse.

Glenn Crouter:
There was a ceremony afterward on the track, and all the jockeys came out to pay tribute to him. I was nearly in tears — in fact, I was holding back a few tears knowing what a tremendous person this guy is and what he's done in his career. You hate to ever see someone's career wind down. When you see Gretzky retire, when you see all these greats retire, you say, "Wow, who's ever going to take their place? Who can take their place?"

Glenn hired someone to pipe me into the party. Then I said a few words and we ate the cake.

Glenn Crouter:
We brought him in with a grand entrance. He didn't want it, but everybody was upstairs having a couple of drinks and waiting for him to come. So it was only natural that when he walked in, it was an entrée, like "Here he comes." He wasn't embarrassed, but it was like he was wondering, "Wow, this is quite something, for this number of people to come and say goodbye to me." You could just see it in his eyes and the way he was reacting.

It was really emotional for us. It was probably one of the tougher days I've ever had to get through — and I've seen a lot of big names retire, but they weren't close to me the way Sandy was starting to become at that time.

Lisa Hawley:
When he came back upstairs for the reception, and we were all there to congratulate him and have some drinks and carry on with the party, you could see he was relieved. He was glad it was over. I looked at him and saw how happy and relieved he was and I thought, "Well, he's got something to look forward to now. That chapter of his life is over."

When I first started out at the racetrack, I wanted to be a jockey, not knowing what was going to be involved. It took a lot of hard work and dedication. A lot of hopefuls try to be jockeys and never get to the point where they become a rider — they decide it wasn't for them after all. Not me. I knew all along that it was for me, that it was what I wanted to do. I had great people behind me — Colin Wick and Duke Campbell — and I worked hard.

Before I rode my first race, I was going around the barn on a horse one morning, and somebody said, "Hey, jock, how are you doing this morning?" Just for someone to call me "jock" made me feel I was coming close to really being there, to riding in my first race. All I wanted to do was get my name in the program, indicating that I had become a jockey. Then, having achieved that, I wanted to be in the top ten on the local circuit. And of course, once you're in the top ten you strive for more, but never in my wildest dreams did I think I'd end up being the leading rider, let alone one of the top riders in Canada — and then North America — for a number of years.

Glenn Crouter:
I've gone to many events and they'd introduce all sort of celebrities and sports heroes, but who probably got the biggest round of applause? Sandy. That shows the guy's staying power. I have never, ever met anybody who had a bad word to say about him or that he burned a bridge. If I'm walking through a grandstand with him at any racetrack in North America, I have to leave him because everybody stops him — and he will not just offer a token handshake. He stops to talk to

everybody. I've seen so many athletes who don't have the time of day for people, but Sandy feels that if somebody gave him the time to come up and say hello, he's obligated to give them the time back.

Looking back at my horse-racing career, I do have some regrets. You always wish you could win a Kentucky Derby, which I never did. And riding Secretariat would have been a dream come true. He was the best horse I ever saw in my career — and in my life to date, in fact — and the best racehorse I'd ever seen race. It would have been a career-capping thrill to have had the opportunity to ride him in his last race. Unfortunately, it didn't materialize. People always ask me, "Who's the best horse you ever rode?" It kind of hurts, because it might have been Secretariat. I'd rather have ridden Secretariat in his last race and won it at Woodbine than win a Kentucky Derby, but a Derby would be a close second.

Otherwise, I have no regrets. People treated me well, and I consider myself fortunate to have had the career I did. So, I really can't complain. Even as I say, "I wish I could have ridden Secretariat" or "I wish could have won a Kentucky Derby," I'm quick to point out that these things would only have made a great career better.

My young sons, having spent so much time around the jockeys' room at a formative age, thought a little bit about becoming riders, but it likely won't happen. Bradley is definitely way too big, and I think Russell will be too big as well. But if they wanted to be jockeys, I wouldn't discourage them at all. I know, of course, how dangerous the sport can be — and I'm glad that Lisa no longer has to worry about me anymore now that I'm retired. I know she wouldn't want the boys to become jockeys. To have to worry about her kids would probably be even worse than having to worry over me. As time has passed, they really haven't shown any interest in learning how to ride. They've been on ponies at the track a few times, but nothing beyond that.

The job I have now allows me to spend more time with my family. When you're riding, it's a busy schedule — you go out in the mornings to exercise horses, then you're getting ready for the afternoon or evening races. Sometimes, it's a seven-day-a-week job. And I'd miss out on Halloween or Easter. Now I can spend those special times with the boys. It's wonderful to be able to go to my sons' school functions and to help them out if I can, and I think my boys appreciate that. My dad was a great father to me, and I want to be just the same for my boys.

I remember when Bradley and Russell first walked, and it was actually me who got them to take their first steps. I was out on the street when they got the training wheels off their bikes for the first time.

Where my racing career is concerned, I think they're getting a better idea of what I did. Sometimes, we'll get stopped at the shopping mall or when we're having dinner at a restaurant, as people come up and say hello or congratulate me on my career. One year, Woodbine made a promotional Sandy Hawley bobblehead doll — actually, I think that made even more of an impression on them than anything! I was very impressed when I saw it — it was quite a good likeness. I was also impressed that Woodbine would want to do that for me. When you think about other athletes and personalities that have been depicted, it's quite a tribute. I never really thought I'd have one of my own. Occasionally, I'm approached by people who want to get their bobblehead autographed.

A few years ago, I was told I no longer had to take the cancer vaccines, but I still undergo CAT scans and ultrasounds — set up by Dr. Lou Teglas, our family physician and the former on-call doctor at Woodbine — every six months. I feel fine and healthy now. Because I've had cancer and I'm a survivor, I've had people call my home and office looking for help — not only about skin cancer, although most of the conversations are specifically related to malignant melanoma, in which case I've referred them to my California specialist, Dr. Malcolm Mitchell. There are good doctors in Toronto who I also refer them to, but Dr. Mitchell helped save my life, so I advise people to call him for a second opinion.

Two of those people happened to be Charles Taylor and his wife, Noreen. Charles, for whom I had ridden South Ocean to victory in the 1970 Canadian Oaks, had been diagnosed with melanoma in 1987 and had been told he had only six months to live because the cancer had metastasized from a spot that was never found to a tissue in one of his thighs. While the tumour was removed, it redeveloped three years later and was discovered after he'd broken a leg.

Noreen Taylor:
We were getting lost in the medical system, and what you needed to hear was "How am I going to stay alive?" or "What's going to happen?" As Charles began fretting more and more, I turned to him and suggested he talk to Sandy, who has melanoma, even though it's a dreadful imposition and he might not want to talk about it. A lot of people don't want to talk about illness — certainly Charles didn't.

I said to Charles, "I just think Sandy would help." In the back of my mind, I thought Sandy would at least say something calming like, "It's okay, I've had it. I'm still here. I'm still riding. I'm still fit," and provide the kind of support that Charles would need and prevent him from feeling quite as alone, facing this obstacle no one could tell us about.

Instead of that, Sandy took Charles under his wing and said, "Yes, it's manageable. Here's the doctor I see, here's what he does, here's the kind of program I go through, here's how it's been working for me." Charles chose not to go through his kind of program because it would have involved our moving to California; he wanted to keep going with the life he had for as long as he could. He didn't want to leave Windfields — that was a large part of it. What would happen to it if he left? The decision he took was to stay in Canada and get the best treatment he could, but he was in contact with Sandy's California doctor, Malcolm Mitchell, for many years. This man was just unbelievably kind in suggesting courses of treatment that Charles would then take to his oncologist, and then they'd work out a program.

I'm not saying Sandy gave Charles an extra number of years — he passed away in 1997 — but he certainly gave him the peace of mind that there was something to be done.

Sandy has never forgotten a friend, and if you were the absolute only man on the street whom he had never met, you'd be his friend. If he has anything he can give to you, whether it's the shirt off his back or information, he's unbelievably generous with that. He's unbelievable generous with his time. Those are qualities you don't find.

The story I told is not the most important part. What's important is that he found the time to be of help. He found the time to make the calls that needed to be made. That's just because he was Sandy, and he'd go to that effort. He's absolutely one of nature's gentlemen.

Through an association with Mrs. Taylor and Tribute Communities, I am now promoting a housing development on a portion of Windfields Farm. It is called The Neighborhoods of Windfields Farm, and it will eventually include 3,000 homes built over a twenty-year period. The first phase is underway, and it will consist of 689 homes built over five years. My family and I will move into one of those homes in 2006. It will be near an area where I galloped horses when I first began my career in the mid-'60s after meeting trainer Duke Campbell. It's also special because I won my last Queen's Plate for Windfields Farm, aboard Regal Embrace in 1978.

Noreen Taylor:
We happen to think it's the most beautiful piece of property in the world, and Sandy, because he knows it and worked there and was in Oshawa as a kid, I think has kind of a romantic attachment to it. It just seems like it made sense. It's one of those things that kind of magically happens. It's just a fit.

When I married Lisa, we bought a home in Mississauga and lived there for several years. Then we moved to Pickering, forty minutes or so to the east. We thought we'd be there for a long time, but then came the opportunity to move to Windfields, and we couldn't turn it down. It's going to be a beautiful subdivision — a landmark place.

I started out in Oshawa, and here I am, more than fifty-five years later, back where I was born. When I left Oshawa, I never thought I was going to end up back there, where my roots are. I think Lisa, our sons and I will all enjoy it. We're closer to Lisa's family and my dad; our new home will be only a ten-minute drive from the place my parents and I lived in on Thickson Road, and it's ten minutes from where Lisa grew up. It's funny how things work out.

If you were to ask me to sum up my life, when I look back on everything, both good and bad, I'd say I had the ride of a lifetime.

CHAPTER TWELVE

Notes, Quotes and Anecdotes

Held Up at Gunpoint

In the spring of 1985, I got the worst scare of my life. At about 9:30 in the morning, somebody knocked at the front door of the house my second wife Vicki and I owned. We lived in a nice neighborhood, just around the corner from the trainer D. Wayne Lukas. I went to the door, looked out and saw a guy with a Members Only jacket — they were in style at the time — over his arm. He was very well dressed, wore sunglasses and had a moustache. I thought he was a salesman or something. I turned off the alarm, not thinking there was any reason to be concerned. I opened the door and the guy pulled back his jacket to reveal a gun that looked like the Magnum Clint Eastwood used in the Dirty Harry movies. He ordered me to "Back up," so I did.

"Is there anyone else home with you?" he demanded to know. I said, "My wife, Vicki, is in the bathroom having a shower, but that's the only person in the house with me."

"We're going to have to go and find her," he said. As we walked down the hall, he was behind me. "I'm not going to hurt you guys, you just co-operate," he said. "I'm a horse-racing fan. Every time I bet on you, you lose. Every time I bet against you, you win. I'm losing my house, and if I lose it, I'll lose my family. I need money and I need money quick. I followed you home a few times and I just need some money right now. I'm never going to do this again, and I won't hurt you guys as long as you co-operate."

Vicki was getting out of the shower and I explained the situation to her. I said, "Vicky, he's a robber, but he said he won't hurt us as long as we co-operate."

He told me I had to tie her up on the floor, so he let her get her housecoat on. He kept the gun pointed at me while I tied my wife up on the floor, then he made me put my hands behind my back and he tied my hands. He ended up hog-tying me, so I was in my housecoat, my wife was in hers, and we were both hog-tied on the floor. He sat on the bed and went through the whole story again, then he started rummaging through the house.

He came back — by this time my wife was upset and crying a bit. I was pretty scared, but I was trying so hard to keep her calm, while at the same time trying not to think about the danger myself. I remember that when he came back, I said, "We need pillows for our heads because we're very uncomfortable here." At one point, my wife looked at my hands because they were beginning to hurt from being tied too tightly. They were turning blue. So he loosened my hands a little bit. When he did things like that, it made me feel a little more comfortable — as if perhaps he wasn't going to rob us and then kill us.

Then he said, "Okay, I've looked through the house. Do you guys have a safe?" We didn't. He said, "I'm looking for something valuable." I said, "My wife's ring is over on the table. It's pretty valuable, you can take that." He went over, took the ring and asked if there was anything else he could take. I said, "I have some trophies and memorabilia in the family room, but I would appreciate if you didn't take them." There was a funny moment then, when my wife said, "Oh, yeah, you tell him to take my ring, but you don't let him take the trophies!" He stole my Order of Canada — I had to write the government and get my medal replaced. It took some time to get it back.

He ended up getting between fifteen and twenty thousand dollars' worth of cash, jewellery and valuables. He said at the end, "I'm going to have to put gags on both of your mouths before I leave because you can't be hollering and screaming when I first leave." I didn't think this was a good sign. My wife spoke up and said she needed a drink of water first; so, he went and got her a drink of water. At that point I said to my wife, "You know, we don't have to worry now. He wouldn't get you a drink of water and then kill us."

He brought back a glass of water, gave us pillows and loosened my hands. Then he walked out the door, down the driveway and I never saw him again.

Before he left, he asked me if I liked any horses I was riding in the future. Imagine — he's just gone and robbed us, and then he wants me to give him a tip!

I got untied in about ten minutes and we called the police right away. They came and dusted the house for fingerprints — they didn't get a thing. They told us that if a guy pulls off a job like this more than once, there's a greater chance they'll get caught. If this was really a one-time thing, it wasn't likely they would catch him.

We gave the police information for a composite sketch, and when it was finished it was remarkable how much it looked like the guy who robbed us. The only disguising features were his moustache and sunglasses. I'm sure he shaved his moustache after the robbery.

They never did catch the guy.

The effects took some time to wear off. For two weeks after the incident, we couldn't sleep in our bed — that's where the guy dumped all the contents that he had stolen from us. The experience was so traumatic. And for a while, anytime someone came to our door, I was afraid it might happen again.

I was riding a horse called Who's Got a Nickel the day after the robbery — I rode the horse on both March 24 and April 6, and I'm not sure exactly which day this was — and somebody called from the grandstand, "Hey, Hawley, have you got a nickel?" My blood ran cold for a moment — I thought it might be the robber. In both instances, I didn't win the race.

The scariest thing that ever happened to me was seeing that gun, and the greatest relief I ever felt in my life was when I heard his footsteps go down my driveway. For some time afterward, I'd be looking over my shoulder, wondering if I might see this guy at the race track. Thankfully, I never saw him again.

Ransom on My Life

In 1973, when I was in Maryland chasing Bill Shoemaker's single-season record of 485 wins, I needed to hire protection because of a threat to kidnap me. These guys were getting out of jail in Toronto and they were going to kidnap me for a ransom. I found out about it in the middle of one day's racing card, when the steward called me in. A steward won't normally call you in the middle of the day — they usually wait for the end or before the next day's card.

I had a race off, so I went in. My agent, Colin Wick, was already there, along with the three stewards. There were also two other guys in suits who wanted to talk with me. They identified themselves as plainclothes policemen, and told me what they had heard. He said the two would-be kidnappers knew everything about my daily routine — when I left for the track, what time I got home, even when I walked my dog. They explained that they had found out after one of the conspirators got out of jail and didn't want to be a part of it. He'd gone to the Metropolitan Toronto Police and tipped them off — I guess so he wouldn't be implicated if anything happened to me.

It scared the crap out of me. The plainclothes guys followed me around for two weeks. They'd be waiting outside my hotel room every morning when I went to the racetrack, they'd follow me home, and they'd watch the hotel room around the clock. My first wife, Sherrie, and I would go out to dinner and they'd watch us from another table. Sherrie and I would bar the door with the couch every night, scared out of our wits that someone might break in and kidnap me. It was a pretty scary two or three weeks, but nothing ever came of it.

Golfing with Dean Martin and the Record that Wasn't

My success in California after the 1975 season brought me into new circles and created some interesting new experiences. One day I golfed in a group that included the singer Dean Martin and Lew Bedell, the president of Doré Records. Lew was a horse owner, and one day, in the paddock after I rode a horse for him, he asked me to come out and play golf with him at the Riviera Country Club. He invited me to bring along one of my jockey friends, and mentioned our fourth would be Dean Martin.

Earlier in his career, Lew Bedell had been a standup comedian, and I thought he was joking now, but I was looking forward to playing the Riviera Club. I can't remember who the jockey was who came along with me, but I remember taking my clubs out of the car and walking up towards the front of the clubhouse. There was a car parked out in front — it was a Stutz Blackhawk, one of those customized Pontiacs — and the licence plate read DRUNKY. Lo and behold, it was Dean Martin's car! I couldn't believe it: I was actually going to play golf with Dean Martin.

And it was a thrill. They were like a comedy team the whole way around. I was betting two bucks a hole, while they'd be betting fifty bucks a hole. I really didn't want the day to end; it was just fantastic. We had a drink with them afterwards and joked around and everything, and then Lew asked me if we could do it again the following Monday. I told him I've love to. What I didn't realize was that the following Monday was a racing day. I couldn't get a hold of Lew because I didn't have his phone number. I had a mount in a stakes race that Monday, and it took precedence — even over golf with a member of the Rat Pack.

Lew came to the races about a week later and said, "Sandy, where the heck were you? Dean Martin and I were on the tee, and you and the other guy didn't even show up."

"Well, Lew," I explained, "I thought you realized that we had to race that day. And I didn't have your number to get a hold of you."

Then he said, "Dean Martin was asking about you, too." Holy cow! He remembered me? "What'd he say?" I asked.

"Dean said, 'When are those two midgets coming back to play golf with us again?'" That was cool.

At some point, Lew suggested to me it would be a good idea if we tried to cut a record together. He asked if I could sing. I said I really couldn't, but he convinced me to come to the studio and give it a try. "I've got this record that we started out to do with some people, but it ended up not panning out." So he would put my voice over the backing track, which included background singers. We ended up cutting two songs, "Dusty, My Darlin'" and "Little Orphan Boy." It was to be a 45, with "Dusty, My Darlin'" on the Aside. Lew was convinced he could get me on Johnny Carson's show. Then he said he wanted me to come up with half the money to release the record. I thought this was odd; he was the record executive, so why wouldn't he assume all the costs?

I wasn't sure, so I called my business manager, Roger Smith, who had taken on some of my financial planning as well as my income grew. He also worked for other Ontario-based riders, and he'd set up a corporation, Sandy Hawley Enterprises Ltd., to handle some of my affairs. He advised me against going ahead with the project. He said it was Lew's record company, and he should put up the whole cost of manufacturing and distributing the record. So, I left it at that. I just said to Lew, "You can put out the record, and I'll go out and promote it if you want me to." He never went ahead with it, so the record never made it to market.

Hanging out with Farrah Fawcett

When I was riding in California in the late '70s and living in Marina Del Rey, I met a young guy named Darryl Goldman, a tennis instructor who loved going to the races. He knew I liked to play tennis, and he offered to teach me. We also played table tennis at the condominium I was renting. He was good friends with the actor Vince Van Patten, who was also a nationally ranked tennis player. He came from an acting family, headed by his father Dick, the star of the television series *Eight Is Enough*. Dick Van Patten also owned racehorses and loved going to the races. In fact, wherever he travelled, he had to stop off at every racetrack along the way.

Darryl told me one day that he had been invited to Dick's house to play tennis, and he asked me to come along as his partner. Vince's partner was Farrah Fawcett-Majors, the star of the television show *Charlie's Angels* and extremely popular at the time because of a sexy poster she'd posed for. I think I played the worst game of my life that day — I couldn't concentrate on the ball. Ha, ha. She was just in the process of getting divorced from Lee Majors, the star of the television show *The Six-Million-Dollar Man*. We became good friends; I have pictures of her with Laffit Pincay, Bill Shoemaker and me in the jockeys' room, and I have another picture of her standing beside me while I stood on the scales.

We used to go out and play paddle tennis at Venice Beach. Darryl, Vince and I kind of hung out there. I wasn't really a big beach person until I met Darryl and Farrah and Vince. They used to go almost every day. They were very down-to-earth people, really a lot of fun. One day, Farrah Fawcett said, "Vince and Darryl can't make it to the beach tomorrow, but I'm going to be down there and read a script. If you'd like to come down to the beach, I can meet you." I was still married to my first wife, Sherrie, at the time, but I couldn't turn down that offer. I didn't say anything or do anything that could be construed as making a move, because I respected who she was and because I was married. It was just a friendly relationship. It was wonderful to know such superstars and know that they can be very good, down-to-earth people.

Don Adams and the Playboy Mansion

Don Adams, the star of the television show *Get Smart*, was a huge racing fan. He also had a quiz show, and he invited me to come see him film some of the episodes. One day he saw me in the paddock and said, "I'm going to the Playboy Mansion tonight and I'd like you to come along." Unfortunately, I couldn't go because Marje Everett, the majority owner of Hollywood Park, was hosting a party that night. Marje really treated me super; she'd take Laffit Pincay, Bill Shoemaker and me to Arizona on our days off. At her parties, I'd met the likes of Elizabeth Taylor, Jimmy Stewart and Burt Bacharach.

I told Don that I had to turn down his invitation because I'd already accepted Marje's — it didn't seem right to cancel on her. Don never invited me to the Playboy Mansion again. Perhaps it's just as well — I was married at the time anyway, so it probably wouldn't have gone over that well.

Meeting Mickey Rooney

During my battle with cancer, Mickey Rooney recommended a doctor, and even though I didn't use the one he suggested, it was nice to have that option on the back burner.

I was first introduced to Mickey when I was an apprentice in Florida in 1970. He was making a presentation at a function. Several years later, when I was riding in California, he remembered that meeting. He leaned over the grandstand railing as I was walked back to the jockeys' room after a race and said, "Hey, Sandy, how you doing? Good to see you again." I could hardly believe he remembered me!

Then, one of the ladies in the crowd called out, "Mickey, how you doing?" She was just thrilled to be able to meet him. And he replied, "Hi, darlin', how you doing?" He was so gracious — and such a smooth talker. No wonder he was such a ladies' man in his day.

It was kind of neat having friends like Mickey Rooney and some of the other stars I met in California. All the actors and actresses I met were so down to earth. You kind of put them on a pedestal, but they're human beings, and the ones I met were very nice, including Mickey Rooney.

Bobby Orr and Me

Though we're about the same age and both spent our formative years in Oshawa, I didn't know Bobby Orr in those days. He attended Oshawa's Catholic Central High School, while I was at Anderson High School in Whitby. I idolized him and to be his friend now is amazing. He hosts an annual golf tournament in Oshawa for the local hospital, and I'm invited every year. He's just a very down to earth guy.

Once, while I was doing television work for Sportsnet, which broadcasts some of Woodbine's racing cards, I interviewed Bobby for a feature segment. The focus was on his playing days in Oshawa, as well as what he was doing at the time, including his involvement in the golf tournament, where the interview took place. It was very easy-going, very friendly, because that's the kind of guy he is.

In 1970, I finished second to him in the voting for Ontario's Athlete of the Year Award, selected by sportswriters and sportscasters. He had 1,110 points — I was a distant second, with 380. That was the year he'd led the Bruins to a Stanley Cup victory, scoring the Cup-winning goal in dramatic fashion, and won most of the big awards in the playoffs. Even to be second to him was quite an honour.

Dressing for the Order of Canada

In October 1976, Sherrie and I travelled to Ottawa to receive my investiture in the Order of Canada. I went to the Parliament Buildings, where I was amongst doctors, scientists and so many top people that had done great things for Canada. I couldn't believe I was in such elite company.

At 11 a.m., the bus was scheduled to come around to the hotel to pick everyone up. At about 10 o'clock I started to get dressed — I'd brought my tuxedo — and when I went to put on my shirt, I couldn't believe it: I'd forgotten my tuxedo shirt! I didn't have anything else that was appropriate, so I ran down to the men's store downstairs and asked the salesman, "Do you sell tuxedo shirts?" He looked at me and said, "I'm sorry, we don't have one that will fit you." I was desperate, so I asked him for the smallest one he had. It fit me okay in the collar, but the sleeves were way too long.

We came up with the bright idea of putting elastic bands around my biceps to hold the sleeves of the shirt up. That whole day, while I waited my turn to receive my Order of Canada, the elastic bands were cutting off the circulation to my arms. For a while, I was reaching over and pulling at one elastic band, then the other, to relieve the pressure.

Losing and Finding Spot

In 1976, while towing the horse trailer she used to transport the show-jumping horses she owned and rode in major North American events, Sherrie stopped off at a gas station in the middle of the Mojave Desert. Out popped a Labrador pup, which had been there for four days without any owner, so Sherrie decided to take care of him. She named him Spot. One night, we were out visiting some friends. As we were leaving — at about 11 o'clock — Spot and our Dalmatian, Sheba, started running because they wanted to go over to the field and pee. I hollered for the dogs to stop because they were running into the path of a taxi. Sheba stopped, but Spot just got clipped by the taxi.

I went over, looking for Spot, expecting him to be right where he'd been hit by the taxi. But he was gone. He'd just kept on running. He had been so freaked out by getting hit by this taxi — and this was the first year that we had him — that he just took off. He disappeared.

We put up posters around the neighbourhood, with our home phone number, and offered a reward of $200. When you lose a dog like that, you're naturally so attached to him that it's like losing a member of the family. I just couldn't stop thinking about it, even when I was riding.

Over the next week, we received a few phone calls people who thought they'd seen the dog, and we actually went to the vet a couple of times, but in every case the dog they'd found turned out not to be Spot. But someone did find him: a school principal, who had taken him to a vet. I offered to give him the $200, but he said, "Instead of that, would you come to my class and talk to my kids about your job?" So I did. I took some of my riding equipment with me and just explained what it's all used for, then described the different jobs you can get at the racetrack.

Almost Lunching with the Queen

In the fall of 1977, I was invited to be one of the guests at a luncheon with Queen Elizabeth at the Skyline Hotel. But I missed it. Sherrie and I went to the Skyline Hotel in Toronto — not realizing that there was a Skyline Hotel in Ottawa, and that was the actual site. I had heard sometime beforehand that the Queen planned to attend a Canadian Football League game in Ottawa, between the Ottawa Rough Riders and Hamilton

Tiger-Cats, but I figured she would attend the luncheon in Toronto and fly back for the game. It was very unfortunate because it would have been one of the thrills of my life.

Sheba the Watchdog

One morning in Maryland, I woke up and saw the daylight shining through the door. "Did you close the door last night?" I asked Sherrie. She said she had closed it *and* locked it.

I got up and found that all the money had been taken from Sherrie's purse, but luckily nothing happened to us. It's pretty scary to think that somebody can come into your place like that — and it wasn't a very big place — and rob you while you're sleeping. We had a Dalmatian pup, Sheba, who was in the room with us, but I guess she wasn't much of a watchdog!

Colin and the Cat

When I came to ride in California in 1975, I shared an apartment with my longtime agent, Colin Wick. One night, Colin had a few drinks and went to the grocery store to pick something up. In front of the store there was someone selling kittens, and Colin bought one and brought it home. Colin's wife, Margaret, was living with us, too, at the time, but when the two of them had to go back to Toronto for a little while, I started taking care of it. The darn thing kept me up every night. He kept crying and crying whenever I left the room. And he always wanted to sleep on my head. Colin and Margaret ended up taking him back to Canada.

The Leg Injury… Sort Of

One day in California, I had a mount in one of the later races, and when my horse was loaded into the starting gate it flipped over backwards and landed right on me. The gate crew was trying to get me out, but they couldn't because the horse was still leaning on me.

Finally, they got the horse back up and laid me on the ground and — honest to God — I thought I'd broke my femur.

My leg was hurting so badly. Wayne Harris, who was riding in the race, jumped off his horse and said, "Are you okay, Sandy? Are you okay?" I said, "Wayne, I think I broke my leg. I think I broke my femur."

They put me in the ambulance — the hospital was actually just across the road. I'd never felt so much pain in my leg before. As soon as I got to the hospital, my leg began shaking like mad. I didn't have a broken leg — it was a muscle spasm! It worked itself out, and I just got up and said, "You know what? I'm okay now." Still, x-rays were taken, and there were no broken bones. My ankle was a little bit sore, but it wasn't bad — I could walk on it.

Platform shoes were popular then, and I had a pair with a bit of a heel. Here I was, walking around with these high-heeled shoes, and I thought it was fine.

Colin and I had already planned a trip to go to Las Vegas, so I told him it was still on. We flew there, and about an hour after our arrival we were standing at the craps table. But my ankle really started to hurt. In fact, I had sprained my ankle and hadn't realized it; it started to swell up, so I had to get the weight off of it. I went upstairs, Colin got me a bucket of ice, and I kept icing it off and on. The next day, we got a set of crutches because I couldn't put any weight on my ankle.

We were to return to California on the second day because I had a mount in a stakes race later that day. I remember trying to put weight on my ankle, and I didn't think there was any way I would be able to ride. The manager of the hotel said, "Colin, you'd better call California and tell them to book Sandy off the mount, because he can't even walk on his ankle."

"No, no," Colin insisted. "He's going to ride today."

When I got on the airplane, I said, "Colin, I don't think I'm going to be able to ride. I can't even put weight on my ankle." And he said, "Oh, I was just joking around with them. But we're going to go and see Dr. Kerlan. I'm not going to take you off your mount yet." Dr. Robert Kerlan was the top orthopedic surgeon in California at the time; he also worked with the Los Angeles Rams football team and basketball's L.A. Lakers. He was also the L.A. Kings' head orthopedist, and the orthopedic doctor for the California jockeys. He loved horse racing; he used to come into the jockeys' room and play cards before the races started.

We got in to see Dr. Kerlan at about 10 o'clock in the morning. Dr. Kerlan looked at my ankle, kind of felt it a little bit, and gave me a needle. He actually put a needle in with a syringe, took fluid out and put cortisone in. I stood up on my ankle and it was like a miracle. I couldn't believe that I could actually walk on my ankle. And Colin had the crutches under his arm, so here he looked like a miracle worker because I had walked into the office on crutches and walked out without them.

To make a long story short, I won the stakes race that day. Unbelievable. Colin was laughing his head off and wondering what the hotel manager in Las Vegas would have thought about it.

Working the Penalty Box in Los Angeles

When I first went to California in the '70s, I wanted to get season tickets for the Los Angeles Kings hockey games. This was before Gretzky had been traded there, when the Triple Crown Line of Marcel Dionne, Dave Taylor and Charlie Simmer were still the main attraction. Jake Milford was the general manager at the time and Jack Kent Cooke was the owner; both were Canadian.

Milford was a racing fan, and I got hold of him and told him I wanted to get season tickets. They didn't really have a lot of fans in those days; the rink might be three-quarters full for most games. He asked me where I wanted my seats, and I ended up getting two in a corner area.

The first year, I went to all the games. I used to take my valet, Jack Wood, all the time. Jack was one of my best friends in California; he was in my wedding party, along with Chris McCarron and John Tyre. I enjoyed the hockey games and cheering on the Kings. I got to know the guy who ran the time clock, Bill Meuris. He was in charge of the off-ice officials, and he also became a good friend.

After the first season, the guy who sat directly behind me said, "Sandy, the two tickets that are beside you are mine as well. I'm letting them go next year. Do you know anyone who might want them?" So I asked Chris McCarron, and he ended up buying them. We'd go to the odd game together with our agents. I was at one game, and Bill Meuris came up to me about five minutes before the opening face-off and said, "Sandy, no pun intended, but I'm short a guy to work in the penalty box tonight. Could you come down and do it?" Of course, my heart started beating as if I were about to ride in the Kentucky Derby.

"Gee, Bill," I said, "I don't know anything about working in the penalty box."

"It's fairly simple," he assured me. "You just write down the time when the guy goes in, and when he gets out, and let him out at the appropriate time." So, I did it. I got to meet a couple of the players and really enjoyed myself.

I told Bill, "Anytime you want me to do it again, it would be a pleasure." He said one of his officials was retiring the next year, so I agreed to do take his place. I let go of my season tickets and worked full time in the penalty box at the Fabulous Forum. Even after I returned to Canada to race full time, there was a standing invitation for me to work in the penalty box at the Kings' game whenever I was in town.

Marty McSorley

Marty McSorley played for the Kings when I was riding in California. In fact, he was included in the Wayne Gretzky trade from Edmonton. Marty was considered an enforcer when he played; since I was working in the penalty box, I therefore got to know him pretty well — he spent quite a bit of time in there. He loves horse racing, and we became good friends. We'd talk and joke around with one another while he served his penalties. One of my other duties was to collect pucks from the dressing room, and sometimes I'd strike up a conversation with Marty there, too.

The first time Lisa ever met him was after we'd gotten engaged. I worked a game, while Lisa sat up in the stands. Marty was penalized two or three times, and after the game I told Lisa it was time to meet Marty. She said, "I don't want to meet that guy. That guy's crazy." But Marty was a different person on the ice than he was in person. He was a tough guy whose job it was to protect Gretzky and a number of his other teammates, so he looked a little wild on the ice. I managed to convince Lisa he was a nice guy off the ice, she relented, and they really hit off. She later said, "That's guy's great. I love that guy." I always said it's a good thing we were engaged at the time. I might have lost her to him!

Meeting Mickey Mantle

Early in my career, I was invited to a sports banquet in New York. Sharing the daïs with me, amongst others, was Mickey Mantle, the legendary New York Yankee centre fielder. I couldn't believe I was sitting at the table as him. This was back when I had long hair and platform shoes with high heels; everyone must have thought I was some kind of hippie from Canada. They introduced me as Sandy Hawley from Oh-*sha*-wa, not *Osh*-a-wa. They made it seem like I was an Indian from up north.

Dave Keon and Frank Mahovlich

When I was growing up and watching hockey, Dave Keon, the captain of the Toronto Maple Leafs, was my favourite player. At one of the first banquets I went to as a head-table guest, Dave Keon was also there. I didn't know about it ahead of time, so all of a sudden I looked over and there he was. I went up to say hello and told him I was a huge fan. He was very cordial.

On another occasion, I was at a golf tournament and Frank Mahovlich, another famous Toronto Maple Leaf from the 1960s, was there. This was after his career had ended. He ended up sitting at the same table as I, and as the evening progressed I mentioned that he had also been my Lisa's favourite player during his days with the Montreal Canadiens. He was such a wonderful man. He signed a program from the tournament, making it out to Lisa. Then, later on, his team won a prize from the tournament; he received a hockey book filled with pictures of old-time stars, including himself. He opened it up to where his picture was and signed *it* to Lisa, too, with the inscription, "Thanks for being such a great fan. All the best, Frank Mahovlich." We still have that book.

I couldn't tell you how impressed I was that he would actually give away his prize. And I wasn't just feeding him a line of bull when I said Lisa was his favourite player. So, when I brought the book home, she was beside herself. Later on, we attended a Special Olympics event in Toronto, and Lisa had a chance to meet him and thank him personally.

Nicholas Campbell

A few years ago, I met Nicholas Campbell, the star of the television show *DaVinci's Inquest*. It was at a speaking engagement at Hastings Park in Vancouver. Nicholas lived in Vancouver, where the show is filmed, and he owns some racehorses there. He's a big racing fan, and when he was in Toronto in 2004 to film the movie *Cinderella Man*, he routinely went to the Woodbine Entertainment Group's downtown restaurant/teletheatre, The Turf Lounge. (The Woodbine Entertainment Group is the new name for the Ontario Jockey Club.) Glenn Crouter, the director of media communications, and I are often at The Turf Lounge to meet sponsors. Nicholas and I ended up becoming friends, and we'd often have lunch together at the restaurant.

I Don't Really Own the Track

Sometime after my retirement from racing, I filmed a commercial with Rick Zeron, a top standardbred driver, for the Ontario Jockey Club, which was renovating Woodbine. In the commercial, I talked about how I'd fixed up the place.

I had nothing to do with the remodelling, of course; the ad was just part of my job to promote racing at Woodbine. But some people got the impression from the commercial that I actually was a part owner of the racetrack. As he entered the track, one person was overheard commenting to one of the stewards: "So, Sandy saved his money pretty well. He even owns a piece of Woodbine." He had to be told, "He doesn't own Woodbine; he just does a commercial for the Ontario Jockey Club."

Drive-In Hi-Jinks

When I first started working at the race track, a bunch of us who worked for Duke Campbell used to like to go to the drive-in theatre. But there were five of us, and we only had money enough to pay for admission and snacks for three. The solution: two of us would sneak in in the trunk of the car. Normally, I was one of them — even though I was the only one who had a car — because I was one of the smallest.

One time, a couple of us had climbed into the trunk when somebody hollered, "Who's got the keys?" Well, it was my car, so of course I had the keys. So there I was, in the trunk, with the car keys. The other guys ended up having to take out the back seat of the car. We ended up missing the first feature.

Tack Room Pranks

Once, there was this guy who used to drink a lot; he'd come to his tack room about 11 or 12 at night and he'd be talking to himself, waking me and my roommate, Louis Hutchison. One night, we decided we'd fix his wagon; we put Vaseline on the doorknob of his tack room. He came home, and we could hear him talking to himself, trying to get in his room, but he couldn't get a grip on the doorknob because of the Vaseline. He then went to the public bathroom.

We wondered what had happened to him, so Louis and I went into the bathroom, where we found him asleep on the toilet. Being the pranksters that we were, Louis and I got a bucket full of cold water and fired it over top of the stall, then raced back to our rooms and jumped back in our beds. About twenty minutes later, we heard the guy going back to his tack room, talking to himself and cursing Louis and me, knowing we were probably the ones who'd thrown the water on him.

The next morning, I was on a horse and Louis was walking around the shedrow, and the guy we pranked said, "You two little troublemakers! I know it was you." We denied it the whole way, of course.

Gerry Cheevers and Colin Wick

When I went to California to ride in 1975, the first thing I wanted to do was go to a Kings game. Tickets were fairly easy to get back then, but I didn't have anybody to go with, because I didn't know anybody. So, I asked Colin to go with me. He isn't a huge hockey fan, but he joined me, and before the game we went to the Forum Club Lounge inside the Forum for a beer.

It was just about time for the game to begin, and Colin had a drink in front of him. I told him we should go to our seats, and he said, "Go ahead. I'm just going to finish my drink and I'll come join you." He ended up staying in the bar for the whole period! I came in during the intermission and asked what had happened. "I've been in here talking to the bartender," he said. "I can see the hockey game on TV." The next period came and went, and he ended up spending the whole game in the bar.

The Kings had played the Boston Bruins; Colin and I knew their goalie, Gerry Cheevers, because he owned horses, and he used to come to Fort Erie every year and speak at the Paddock Club, where he interviewed some of the riders and trainers. He asked me to join him a number of times. Colin became good friends with him, too, and they used to have some drinks together.

Colin and I stuck around the Forum Club after the game for something to eat, and Gerry Cheevers came walking in. He came over to see us. "So how'd you enjoy the game?" Gerry asked Colin.

"Who was playing?" Colin replied.

"I was, you idiot!"

Can you believe it? Wicksey was actually at the game, and he didn't know Gerry Cheevers was playing. You'd think he'd put two and two together that, when Cheevers comes walking into a bar at a hockey arena, he was probably playing that night.

Reggie Fleming the Hot-Walker

Reggie Fleming was one of the toughest pro hockey players in the 1960s and '70s, and I got to know him in Chicago when I was riding at Arlington Park. Jerry Calvin was a trainer whose horses I rode, and one day I was in the kitchen and he said to me, "I've got this guy walking horses for me and he said he'd like to meet you. He's a Canadian and an ex-hockey player." I asked his name, and Jerry said, "Reggie Fleming."

Wow — that was a name from the past. I remember watching hockey with my dad when Reggie Fleming played for the Chicago Blackhawks.

He had long since retired from the game, and he was hot-walking to get some exercise. I started hanging out with him; we had breakfast with him every morning and went to dinner quite often as well. In Chicago, everybody knew him. We became very good friends.

The Gomez Leap

The late Avelino Gomez made famous the practice of leaping out of the irons with his hands in the air, something that was copied in later years by the likes of Angel Cordero Jr. and Frankie Dettori.

Avelino was my idol, and six months into galloping horses in the morning I decided to try it. I walked a horse in the stall — Gordie Colbourne, who worked for Duke Campbell, was there. I told him to hold onto the horse while I tried to do a Gomez jump. Gordie asked me if I was really ready to do it, and I assured him I was. I leaped in the air and everything went well — except my feet stayed in the stirrups and I got hung up. Gordie helped me out of the stirrups, and that experience left me with even more admiration for the great talent of Avelino Gomez. I persisted, and I had it perfected by the time I did it after winning the Queen's Plate in 1971 with Kennedy Road.

Northern Dancer

When I began learning to ride young horses at the National Stud Farm in Oshawa in 1968, Northern Dancer was active as a stallion there. The farm manager, Peter Poole, took me to see the Dancer one day, but he warned me not to put my hand in the stall because Northern Dancer was feisty. It's fairly common when horses turn to stud duties that they get even more feisty because they're a little more keyed up.

I recall that he was just a little horse, but the talent he had displayed as a racehorse was still evident to me — he had that fire in his eyes. I've often been asked if I rode Northern Dancer, and of course the answer is no because he retired in 1964 and I didn't begin riding until 1968. He was moved to the United States to make him more available for commercial use early into my racing career.

Myrtle Irene

A few years before I retired I rode a horse called Myrtle Irene, trained by Dave Brown, with whom I'd won the Canadian Oaks in 1972 with Happy Victory.

Myrtle Irene was one of my favourite horses to ride because she was so game. She always put out 100 per cent. To be able to win races for Dave was really a thrill, and Myrtle Irene was one of the best horses he had in his career. It was an interesting time in my career. Business was a little bit slow, but to have a filly like her to ride was really exciting. Her owners, Mr. and Mrs. Don McClelland, were also her breeders. They ran a small operation and they really loved horse racing, so it was great to win for them, too. If you got beat on the filly, they didn't blame the rider, because they realized that's part of racing.

Dave Brown knew Lisa was pregnant and he said, "If you have a girl, why don't you name her Myrtle?" Lisa had quite a laugh about that. We'd already picked out the name Britney.

Playing Cards with the Guys

For about ten years I've been playing cards once a month with a group of racetrackers that includes Lou Cavalaris, Jim Bannon, Dave Borsk, Ronnie Robinson, Coffee John Calleja, Al Crost, Dr. Lou Teglas and Darren Gomez, the nephew of the late Avelino Gomez. We meet in different places and usually play poker, or a variation of it.

We just have fun, tell jokes and stories and exaggerate the truth. It's mostly for the camaraderie.

Teaching My Father-in-Law the Business

In 1990, my future in-laws, Isaac and Monica John, came to Kentucky to visit Lisa and me while I was riding at Keeneland Racecourse. Isaac thought my job was dangerous, and he knew jockeys had to work hard, but at the same time he was under a misconception about how much time we put in. He said, "I know it's dangerous, but you make pretty good pay for the length of time you're on the track."

That prompted me to suggest he accompany me on "a day in the life of a jockey," and he agreed. I woke him up first thing in the morning, at about 5:30, and we were at the track by six. I did morning workouts and got on about four or five horses and finished at about 9:30, 10 o'clock. He kept watching the odd workout and reading the *Daily Racing Form*. We went back home and had breakfast, and I told him he could lie down for an hour before we had to leave again for the track and be in the jocks' room by noon. I rode in about seven or eight races, while he spent his time doing his handicapping.

When the day was over, we went back home, had some supper and enjoyed the evening. And by 9:30 or 10 that night it was time to go to bed. The next day we went through the whole routine again. On the third day, when I went to wake him up, he said, "No, no, I understand. I see what you're saying now." He realized it was a tough job after all.

Facts About Sandy Hawley's Career

Born: April 16, 1949, Oshawa, Ontario

Lifetime Record

- 31 years (1968–1998)
- 31,454 mounts
- 6,449 wins
- 4,825 seconds
- 4,158 thirds
- $88,666,071 in purse earnings

Noteworthy Years

1969   North America's top apprentice

1970   Continent's leading race-winning jockey with 452 wins; wins first Queen's Plate and first Canadian Oaks

1971   Wins second Queen's Plate and second Canadian Oaks

1972   Leads continent with 367 wins; wins third Canadian Oaks

1973   Sets a world record for victories with 486, shattering a twenty-year-old mark, and finishes with 515 overall; wins fourth Canadian Oaks; wins the Lou Marsh Award as Canada's outstanding athlete; receives special Eclipse Award of Merit

1974   Wins record fifth consecutive Canadian Oaks

1975   Dominates Hollywood Park meet in first full-time try in California; wins third Queen's Plate

1976   Wins the Eclipse Award as top jockey in North America; leads continent in wins for the fourth time; receives second Lou Marsh Award; is invested in the Order of Canada for outstanding accomplishments by a Canadian citizen

1978   Wins fourth Queen's Plate; wins first Sovereign Award as Canada's most outstanding jockey

1986   Is inducted into Canada's Horse Racing Hall of Fame and wins Woodbine's Avelino Gomez Memorial Award for contributions to racing

1988   Receives second Sovereign Award as Canada's outstanding jockey

1992   Is inducted into the National Museum of Racing's Hall of Fame

Records and Feats

- tied with Robin Platts and Avelino Gomez for most Queen's Plate victories (four)
- holds record for most Canadian Oaks victories (eight)
- captured eighteen Woodbine riding titles, thirteen at Fort Erie meets, nine at Greenwood, nine in Ontario and eight in Canada
- four North American titles (1970, 1972, 1973, 1976)
- retired eighth all-time in career wins
- inducted into nine separate Halls of Fame